PRAISE FOR

More or Less: Essays from a Year of No Buying

In this lively collection of essays, Susannah Q. Pratt observes the culture of middle-class consumption from a pause in her own participation. This pause allows her to consider how our lives are "both confined and defined" by the things we own. The resulting meditation on want, need, excess, and garbage asks profound questions about waste, time, and the lost art of thrift.

— Eula Biss, *Having and Being Had*
and *On Immunity: An Inoculation*

With vivid writing and beautiful imagery, Susannah Pratt has brought the beyond into view, unveiling what was once hidden. The essays in *More or Less* will open you up and move you, asking you to reach for a promising new way of seeing and therefore being in the world. These essays will give you new ways of thinking and talking about consumerism and late capitalism. Each essay is engaging and beautiful.

—Andrew Root, *The Grace of Dogs*
and *Churches and the Crisis of Decline*

It's not every book that can captivate the imagination with the emotional meaning of a son's basketball shoes! And who among us does not relate to a couple's attempt to get a grip on the basement—a tender understanding that the memories held by the objects we own but rarely see may be more powerful than we had thought. I came away from reading this book with a different point of view on the things we fill our lives with.

—Walter M. Robinson, *What Cannot Be Undone*
and judge for the EastOver Press Prize in Nonfiction

More OR Less

Essays from a Year of No Buying

❧❧

SUSANNAH Q. PRATT

More or Less: Essays from a Year of No Buying

SUSANNAH Q. PRATT

© 2022
ALL RIGHTS RESERVED.

ESSAYS

ISBN 978-1-934894-76-7

❧

BOOK DESIGN: EK LARKEN
COVER IMAGE: LUCREZIA CARNELOS (*UNSPLASH*)

Lyrics from "Ill with Want" (2009) by The Avett Brothers,
used with permission.

❧

EastOver Press encourages the use of our publications in educational settings.
For questions about educational discounts, contact us online:
www.EastOverPress.com or info@EastOverPress.com.

PUBLISHED BY

EASTOVER
— PRESS —
Rochester, Massachusetts
www.EastOverPress.com

For John
More, always

We come to hold our dearest possessions
more closely than we hold our friends.
We carry them from place to place,
often at considerable expense and inconvenience;
we dust and polish their surfaces
and reprimand children for
playing too roughly in their vicinity—
all the while, allowing memories to invest them
with greater and greater importance....
But, of course, a thing is just a thing.

AMOR TOWLES, *A GENTLEMAN IN MOSCOW*

❧

I don't want to sell anything, buy anything,
or process anything as a career.
I don't want to sell anything bought or processed,
or buy anything sold or processed,
or process anything sold, bought, or processed,
or repair anything sold, bought, or processed.

LLOYD DOBLER, *SAY ANYTHING*

Contents

INTRODUCTION

When, during my adolescence, my middle-class parents found themselves ascending to the upper-middle class, my mother resisted. Reluctant to embrace her new reality, she modeled for us an almost pathological restraint. Requests for brand name clothing were dismissed out of hand, and she took most every opportunity to remind us that our good fortune was not to be counted upon. To underscore this point, she would engage us in worst-case scenario planning, sprinkling dinner conversations with questions like: "What do you think we would sell first if Dad lost his job?" Or, "I have been thinking... could we manage with just one car?" My father, who was, for the record, consistently employed, would smile and shake his head at her.

My sister and I, however, took the bait. We would think together about what we could "get by on," agreeing to return to a shared bedroom if need be, or thinking through where we could hypothetically hock our TVs. Encouraged by my mother, we discussed what we would save from a fire, how much cash we'd grab if forced from our home, and what jobs we, as 11- and 13-year-olds, could get if we needed to contribute to the family income. Raised in a different time and place, my mother would have made a great prepper. Even today there is a closet in her suburban home filled with emergency supplies – fresh water, canned goods, batteries, and a crank radio. Oh, and a hatchet. Just, you know, in case.

Thanks to this upbringing, throughout my life I have been drawn to those who harbor suspicion about excess – people who do not assume plenty to be a natural state of affairs. My neighbor, raised in a family of eight, once related a story of restraint so compelling that I took to it as though it were my own. During a childhood trip to New Hampshire, she recalls her mother buying a small package containing four maple sugar candies. So potent was the sugary goodness of every bite, her mother explained, that this one box of four candies would suffice for their entire family. My neighbor reports no one argued when her mother broke the candies in half and laid them on the children's expectant tongues. What she remembers instead is closing her mouth and savoring the sensation of the maple candy melting within.

Inspired by this appropriated memory, I instituted a similar policy and told my three boys, toddlers at the time, that a single-serving bag of M&Ms was meant to last an entire week. Each night at dessert time I doled out four round chocolate candies per boy. A swap meet ensued until each secured their preferred colors, gobbled them up and then, completely satisfied, hopped down from their chairs and ran off to play. That the bag was designed to be eaten by one person in a single sitting never once occurred to them.

Though my three (now teenage) boys might argue otherwise, restraint is fundamentally different from deprivation. With restraint, choice is implied and so, it follows, is a baseline of power and privilege: I have and I may therefore choose to stop having, or to have less. Voluntary exercises in restraint can thus seem like the province of the fortunate and clueless. It's one thing to fantasize about giving up a car and using public transportation, it's another thing to stand outside on the train platform in the subzero wind of a gray Chicago dawn. When going without is not optional, things look different. Viewed from the El platform, my mother's scenarios or my candy parsimony can seem like the worst kind of playing poor.

On the other hand, when asked with sincerity, the question of restraint is entirely counter-cultural and powerful enough to be a foothold in our slow societal climb toward equity. Choosing to go with less in a culture committed to "having it all" is not just revelatory, it's revolutionary. Imagine what it might mean for the distribution of resources if those of us with plenty could learn to say, "Thanks, we have enough." It might mean less plastic in the ocean. It could deliver a serious blow to white privilege. Nothing less is at stake.

Mindful of both these issues, in 2018 our family signed on for a year of no buying. After a series of deliberative conversations in the weeks leading up to the start of the year that included – no joke – a PowerPoint presentation that I made and presented to my own family, we undertook a 365-day moratorium on the purchase of new clothes, toys, games, books, electronics, gear, furniture, housewares, and other things that fall in the general category of "stuff. For 12 months we purchased only essentials – food, toiletries, light bulbs, and a few pairs of shoes for my growing boys. We stayed out of stores and off of online shopping sites. We fixed things. We made things. We went without.

We were hardly the first family to do this. Author Ann Patchett documented her year without shopping in an essay for *The New York Times* in 2017 and many people immediately followed suit. "Look," I showed my family in my PowerPoint, "lots of people are doing this. And are HAPPY about it." My PowerPoint also contained a picture of five square miles of plastic trash floating off the coast of Honduras, and a bar graph of our family's annual spending by category. Hard to say which was more stunning or stomach turning.

My slide deck didn't quite connect the dots. Was my plan an effort to save money or the planet? An attempt to clean out or an attempt to find joy? It wasn't clear because *I* wasn't clear. There had been so many factors driving my desire to take my family on this journey: a friend pointing me to a minimalist blog; my children's dresser drawers, overstuffed and unable to close despite the bags of outgrown clothes I regularly dropped at Goodwill; my increasing sense that climate change is a very personal problem. Its deeper roots lay in values instilled in me by my parents and a life of intermittent churchgoing, as well as annual summer trips to a mountain lake which remind me that there is a different way to be.

More than anything else, though, it was this: over the past few years, I had begun to feel oppressed by our stuff. The care, cleaning, and storage of the items accumulated by our dual-income family of five was taking far too much of our time. But the other option, to treat our goods poorly as though they were all ultimately disposable, didn't feel right either. We were caught in a trap; spend time taking care of too much stuff, or fail to care for said stuff and buy more stuff to solve the problem. Once I began to see our choice in these terms, the weight of our things got heavier and heavier. It was with this logic that I convinced my family to shut off the spigot of incoming items. Within days of implementing our decision, I experienced a great sense of relief. Nothing new was coming at me – nothing that had to be removed from packaging, assembled, completed, accessorized, displayed, used, cleaned, folded, stored, repaired, replaced, recycled, thrown out, or donated. I felt free.

As for the rest of my family? They withheld judgement a little longer. Under the terms of our agreement, the boys were allowed to spend their own money. Because of this, while I enjoyed the immediate effects of less stuff, their lives were at first unchanged. Until they weren't. And my husband, perhaps the most joyful consumer in our band of five, initially felt constricted and constrained by our decision. Until he didn't. Eventually they, too, realized the quiet liberation that results from less stuff and more time.

As already observed, no writing about these sorts of en-

deavors – essay or otherwise – is complete without the acknowl-
edgment that exercises like this are a response to privilege. The
challenges I describe here fall cleanly in the "cry me a river"
category. Many people around the globe go without life's most
basic necessities. My biggest problem is not that I have too many
hand towels; to name it even as bothersome is a luxury.

Despite this truth, I remain convinced that the privileged
problem of material accumulation is nonetheless a problem.
As Patchett observes in her essay, there is a reason each of the
major world religions instruct their followers to detach from the
material as they seek the divine. In my own tradition, Christi-
anity, Jesus raises this point again and again. I used to dismiss
these verses, reading them primarily as admonitions about greed
or a misplaced desire for things material over and above things
spiritual – problems I did not perceive myself to have. What I
have come to believe instead is that when it comes to material
goods desire is just the tip of the iceberg. It is actual acquisition
that clutters not just our space but our souls. Before we realize
it is happening, our goods command our energy and attention,
become the organizing force behind our lives, and we thus confer
upon them greater and greater importance. "But, of course,"
explains writer Amor Towles, "a thing is just a thing."

Acquisition is not just a personal problem. Our consumerism lies at the heart of global challenges – vast inequities, a
warming planet. If I am convinced of one thing now, more than
at the start of our year, it is that we got into this gigantic mess
together and we are going to need each other to get out. While
the decisions I describe in this book are primarily my own (and
my family's), each entangles me in a larger web. Where an object
was made, how it got to me, what I do with it when I am done;
none of this is my problem alone. It took a year of me standing outside the system, looking in, to see this. It will take me a
lifetime to figure out how to respond. I am still trying to connect
the dots.

I offer these essays as a first response, a conversation start-er. Anyone reading for a solution will be disappointed. Taking an occasional shopping break is not going to save us. Any redemp-tion here comes not from materials reused or money saved, but from a slow awakening. From learning to parse out and discrim-inate between different levels of desire. From recovering an abili-ty to create and to receive. From acknowledging that one family's effort to change is both wholly inadequate and the only real place to start.

WOMEN'S WORK

The first book assigned to the budding feminist college freshmen in my "Women, Work and Society" seminar was Arlie Hochshchild's *The Second Shift*. Published in 1989, this groundbreaking sociological study documented that despite increased representation in the workforce and marriage to more progressive partners, women were still doing a disproportionate share of the domestic work. Although their husbands might help with the laundry or assist in meal preparation or clean up, women were carrying the mental and physical burden of meal planning and execution (including grocery shopping), childcare arrangements and transportation, family health care, homework help, enrollment in camps and classes as well as logistical follow-through, house cleaning and maintenance, and laundry. Hence, their second shift.

My initial encounter with Hochschild's findings was enhanced by our professor, a harried academic in her mid-forties. A working mother herself, she provided the color commentary. Standing in front of us reading portions of the book aloud with real emotion, she braved the impassive disinterest of a group of undergrads who understood little about the realities of a woman in the workforce, let alone the academy, and were distracted instead by their plans for the upcoming night. Hypothetically speaking, of course.

Hochschild's work lingered in my mind and became one lens through which I have come to view my marriage. Let me say here that I am in most important ways half of a truly egalitarian partnership. But as many since Hochschild have documented, even in households led by the most progressive of couples, married women in dual-income, opposite-sex partnerships continue to do more of the domestic work. Given this, it should come as no surprise that when I shared our decision to forego shopping for a year, my biggest supporters were women.

Our experiment made for interesting dinner conversations, and once the word spread about what we were up to, people wanted to talk. These conversations – especially among married couples – typically began with a diagnosis of which partner was more responsible for the influx of clothes, gear, or housewares. I heard about men with an obscene number of shoes and wives with book buying problems. Despite some initial finger-point-ing, most couples came to quick consensus on which of them was more likely to add to the family larder – the buyer owning it gleefully (gluttony being one of the happier sins), the minimalist shaking their head in resignation. In my own brief sociological study of this topic, I'd say the desire to acquire appears to be gender-neutral, affecting both men and women equally.

But once the goods are in the house? Ah, therein lies the difference. As we began to discuss our experiment, a man would often affirm our choice, noting that an exercise like this would be exactly in line with his value system. But not once did I encoun-ter a man who connected with the exercise viscerally the way his female counterpart did. Women immediately, almost instinc-tively, seemed to understand what I was up to. When I would explain our decision, female listeners would often gasp, turn toward me mouth agape, and nod wide-eyed, hanging on every word. When I referenced the box of empty glass vases that sur-vived two moves without ever having been opened, or redundant purchases of lint rollers (we owned three) or candle snuffers

(inexplicably, two), I would get a kind of call-and-response affir-
mation, a chorus of amens from my sister cleaners and sorters.
No more incoming crap? Preach!

Like children's healthcare or the meal prep documented
by Hochschild, the ongoing care of household goods in most
American families still falls primarily to women. A slew of recent
studies conducted by institutions ranging from the Pew Research
Center to the American Time Use Survey confirm and also attempt to explain this phenomenon. First, it is not in our heads.
These studies document that not only do women perceive themselves to be doing more of the housework, they are actually
doing it. If you're in the mood for some serious self-pity, ladies,
spend a few hours swimming around in this kind of data: according to recent Bureau of Labor Statistics numbers, women, on
average, do 2.3 hours of housework a day as compared to men's
1.4 hours. In recent years, more nuanced studies have broken
down the notion of "housework" to look closely at its various
dimensions: cooking, childcare, and cleaning. And while there
have been some important gains made in male participation
in childcare and cooking, house cleaning still appears to be left
primarily to women.

Here at home, the data resonate. Aside from basic surface
cleaning, in my own family and those of many of my friends, it
is the female head-of-household who takes on the processing of
our things. She is the one who combs through dresser drawers
to remove ill-fitting items. She is the one who insists, finally,
that a linen closet be cleaned out and threadbare towels thrown
away or taken to Goodwill. A fellow mom of three boys sends
her brood on an annual weekend camping trip during which
she does nothing but stay home and purge old clothes, toys, and
books.

The female head-of-household also typically thinks about
where and how to store everything, both temporarily and in the
longer-term; as women, we are in charge of all putting-away.

I can't tell you the number of moms I know who have tried the experiment of leaving something – say a sleeping bag – in the same space on the floor in which it was dropped in a fit of post-sleepover exhaustion. The results of this silent standoff are almost always the same; it will eventually be the mother who removes the item and returns it to its rightful place. But it doesn't feel great to put away dirty things. So it is that she ends up cleaning the dust from the blades of the little oscillating fan, before stashing it in the basement for its winter sojourn.

Sociologists have inquired as to why this gender gap around the cleaning and care of our things stubbornly persists. The primary culprit appears to be societal expectations. In one study, participants were shown a picture of a living room and were informed of the gender of the person living there. When shown a clean room and told that it belonged to a woman, participants were more likely to say it could be cleaner, and she would probably be uncomfortable having visitors over. When shown a picture of a *messy* room and told that it belonged to a man, participants conjectured that he would probably be just fine having people over. Spaces occupied by men are allowed to be messy. When a woman is present, they are not.

Societal expectations are a tricky thing to address. They are deeply psychologically ingrained. They elude policy solutions. The horizon for change is far off. Many of these articles conclude with the recommendation that we model different behavior for our children, suggesting that for my generation, all is already lost. Jessica Grose, in writing on this topic for *The New Republic* in 2013, offers that one immediate strategy might be for women to lower their "filth threshold." But this, she notes, is difficult to do, especially when there are children in the picture. "Did I really need to clean up the house for my father-in-law?" she asks. "Would he have cared if there were a few glasses sitting out on the kitchen table? Probably not. But it's hard to stomach this fix once you have children and the threat of a Fisher-Price hellscape is perpetually around the corner."

If women are the ones who clean, sort, store, and discard, the great irony is that before all that, we consume. According to recent data from Bloomberg, "If the consumer economy had a sex, it would be female." Women drive 70-80% of all consumer purchases which means "that even when a woman isn't paying for something herself, she is often the influence or veto vote behind someone else's purchase." As those tasked with keeping tabs on the household goods, we are the ones most likely to identify, and therefore fill, perceived gaps. We are the ones who notice when the sleeves on our child's raincoat are heading way north of their wrists, and the first to know when the rice cooker breaks. This is the way that, 70-80% of the time, women become the gatekeeper for the material goods that enter our homes.

"...there are days," writes poet Mary Oliver, "I wish I owned nothing." This, I understand. As the female head of our household, I can see now that our year of no buying was my attempt to launch myself from this hamster wheel of consumption and care, to stop working my second shift. If I couldn't change what society expected of me, or what I therefore expected of myself, I could at least control how much I felt responsible for. Sure, we still had lots of stuff to manage, but the fact that we were not adding to that amount relieved a great deal of stress. Stress, I should add, that had been almost entirely self-imposed. No one else in my family cared too much about whether or not the sleeping bag ever made it back into its sack and into the closet. But I did. I did because, while I don't like mess in our common space, I also knew that in a week's time someone was going to come looking for the sleeping bag, and it would help if I knew exactly where to find it.

And here we arrive at the other, understudied, culprit – not so much societal expectations as interpersonal ones. In my house, I am the primary custodian of the things we own, and I mean this in both senses of the word. I am the caretaker; the one

who knows an item's status, whereabouts, and quantity. And as
with anything that is in my custody – children, dog, tortoise, teakettle – I am constantly attending to its overall well-being. I am
also my family's custodian in the other sense, the janitorial one.
For a host of complicated reasons that I am not sure any of us in
my family understand, could easily articulate, or have actively
chosen, I am the person charged with cleaning and maintaining
the space in which all of us and our possessions exist. Extend
the logic of either one of these roles to the thousands of objects
in our home, and you will understand why I wanted less. Why I
wanted, at least for a little while, to clock out.

Banished to the Basement

In economic terms, utility is the total satisfaction we derive from a good. Marginal utility is the increase in satisfaction we get with each additional unit of that good that we purchase. A rational consumer is a utility maximizer.

John and I are cleaning out the basement. It's not for the faint of heart, the basement. Unless built with a finished rec room, circa 1980 or later, most houses where I live have older basements that exist in a cobwebby state of perpetually unfinished Man Cave. It is often possible to tell the exact point when the person who had been trying to make the basement more livable decided to stop and take on another, above-ground project. In our basement, it's the moment they ran out of the bright red paint they had been using to coat the pipes and door jambs, and slapped on some sky blue to cover the last few lengths of pipe.

Most basements, including ours, are dirty. Our basement's ceiling is part of its "unfinished" charm, and every time our son Elliot jumps down the last three stairs to the first floor (which is to say, every time Elliot comes downstairs), a small shower of dust and silt filters through the floorboards above to coat the basement with a fine layer of dirt. Basements in Chicago are also prone to flooding which results in a mildew-esque "basement smell" instantaneously recognizable to anyone who grew up in basement country.

Once basement owners abandon the illusion of any real livability, basements convert to in-home storage units filled with old furniture, toys, and semi-salvaged kitchen appliances. These household items filter down, like the dirt from above, to gradually coat the floor – making safe passage difficult. John and I have noticed that we can no longer easily chart a path across the main room of our basement to his workbench in the back corner. A dust-covered cat carrier, two outdated booster seats, and the thermos from a defunct coffeemaker are blocking the door. And it only gets worse from there. So, we have put on our old clothes and waded in.

The first half-hour is a type of spelunking. We wait for our eyes to adjust to the dim as we shift our junk around, stopping occasionally to remember and exclaim. Each time I surface a new item, I am amazed at the massive testament to procrastination all this junk is, and I marvel that we didn't just skip the storage phase and throw things immediately in the trash. And then, as we stand there sorting through our stuff, it occurs to me that all this accumulation is perhaps the result of avoiding exactly that – the complicated act of putting an item of substance in the garbage.

୶ଢ଼ଢ଼

For a brief period I was in charge of the donation box at my boys' preschool. The large green wooden box, itself a donation from a woodworking father, had a hinged lid and fit snugly in a corner of the hallway outside one of the classrooms. As coordinator of the Outreach Committee, it was my job to empty the box each Friday and take the contents to one of several designated local nonprofits – an affordable housing organization, a domestic violence shelter.

It did not take long for people to discover the box, or for me
to begin to dread Friday mornings. The families at our preschool
filled the box like it was their job. I would regularly come upon
the donation box overflowing with discarded goods, its hinged
lid completely ajar. Despite the large signs requesting clean
items and complete sets, we received: games in squashed boxes
with their remaining pieces sliding out the side; toddler sneakers
tied together in a tangle of frayed and knotted laces; and various
components of sippy cups and lids, none of which fit together.
I was standing in the hallway next to Celeste, our preschool's
beloved administrator, when we discovered that someone had
donated a used toilet brush, discreetly covered up in its matching blue plastic stand. "That's it," said Celeste with finality, while
I donned some latex gloves to remove it, "we are shutting this
thing down."

Anyone who has ever worked a rummage sale or sorted
through donated clothes can tell similar tales. It is entirely
possible to become outraged at the perceived laziness and apathy
of the donor, to wonder what on earth could have been going
through her mind. I think I know exactly what is going through
her mind, and I'm not sure it's apathy at all. It is, I would ven-
ture, a kind of deep, misguided optimism. It takes some effort
to bring a toilet brush into a preschool for donation. It would be
easier, much less embarrassing, and much more cynical to stick
it right in the garbage. Placing that brush in the donation box
was, I believe, a little act of social responsibility laced with some
willing suspension of disbelief. Surely, the donor thought hopefully, someone else could use this now that we are done with it?

Use matters. It is, arguably, the value consumers care most
about – a value that advertisers trade on. Items are touted as
"long-lasting" or "durable," and we are conditioned to think only
about their present and future utility, thus making our purchasing decisions accordingly. To see this notion taken to the
extreme, one need look no further than the concept of planned

obsolescence – the intentional phasing out of a product by its maker. Manufacturers and marketers working under this mandate don't just tout use, they set its terms. My old cell phone was still receiving calls and texts when it would no longer mate with any of the new and functional chargers in my house. Despite my still being able to "use" it for its central purpose, it was on its way to becoming obsolete. I was, explained the cheerful salesperson at my local Apple store, on borrowed time. I would need a new one.

The problem with this limited definition of use is that most of our items exist long beyond their viability, ending up in the garbage but not disappearing. And the worst part? The same adjectives – long-lasting, durable – continue to apply once the item arrives at a landfill. It is this final part of the arc, the part that comes after use, that we choose to ignore at the point of purchase. Conditioned by the market, and governed by the economic notion of utility, we behave "rationally" as consumers, and then oh-so-irrationally when left holding the goods. This is the story of how a toilet brush ends up in the donation box.

The chance for us to think about this final part of the arc – the part that follows use – is, strangely, right at the point of purchase. I could ask myself if the item I am about to buy is made of material that can eventually be repurposed. I could ask if I believe it will continue to function long enough to be meaningfully passed down when I am done with it. I could ask if I really need to buy the item, or, in fact, if I could perhaps borrow something like it or use something I already have. My family was asking none of those things. Instead, we were asking things like: Where can I get the best price on this? And what other colors does it come in?

❧◦❧

After an hour in the basement, I come across a cache of plastic toddler toys that includes a beloved music table. With oversized piano keys, and red and blue lights that flash in time with the music, the table was beloved by our boys. Over an eight-year stretch, the toddlers in our house pounded and drooled on it, and smashed Cheerios between its keys. Standing at the table, they hammered out their tunes, bobbing and swaying to the sounds they created.

After years of use in our house, the little music table fell silent. Banished to the basement, it has lingered in the limbo of my own wishful thinking. My own misguided optimism. I hold it up for John to see, and we smile as we try to wrap our minds around the fact that our boys were once small enough to stand at the table and play. I press on the keys, gummy from layers of grime made worse by years of basement dwelling. I can barely depress them; they make only a dull thud if they make any noise at all. I look at John and we agree: it is no longer a matter of new batteries or careful cleaning. The thing is simply broken beyond repair and can't be handed down or recycled, no matter how much we want to assign it this fate. There isn't a donation box on this planet that I can in good conscience leave it in. With a slightly sick feeling, I empty the table of its corroding batteries, carry it upstairs, and drop it in our garbage can for pick-up later in the week.

෫ঙ৯

What if there were another way to think about utility; one that takes into account the weight of my sick feeling and thereby discounts my overall satisfaction derived from the good? Better yet, imagine an economic theory in which consumer satisfaction is not the primary reference point. I am craving a definition of rational choice that is not about maximizing my happiness but also protecting the earth. For real sustainability, I suspect, we are either going to have to decenter our current notion of utility or find a way to expand it beyond ourselves.

I am thinking about this as I make my way back down the

stairs to rejoin John in the basement, our Sea of Utility, flooded with all the items for which we once had use. He is seated on the floor near the workbench, sifting through a crate of old CDs. I can tell from his posture, and the activity in which he is now engaged, that he has given up. We will not be cleaning anymore. It's all too much. I clear a space on the ground next to him and take a seat. We lift the cracked cases out of the box, smiling over past concerts and forgotten songs. As the dust dances around in the slanting rays of the afternoon sun, we sit there on the cold basement floor, swirling in the eddies of our memories and drowning in the piles of our things.

PARSING DESIRE

It isn't normal to know what we want.
It is a rare and difficult psychological achievement.
— *Abraham Harold Maslow*

"Oh," say people who hear about our decision to refrain from shopping for a year, "how great. So, like, you'll just be buying the things you need."

Yes, it would seem. Though I am no longer sure.

❧

My in-laws are fond of recalling how, as an adolescent, my husband was expert at making a case for his "needs." Among the items he "needed" were an Atari, a Ralph Lauren polo shirt, and a hot tub. His own father, Howard, grew up on the shores of Lake Superior in the small town of Grand Marais. Howard's father, Harry, the town dentist, passed away when Howard was eight. From that time forward, Howard, his brother, and his mother lived off of her first grade teacher's salary until the boys were old enough to contribute to the household income. It is not surprising to me that John's pleas for a hot tub went unheard.

My husband's adolescent self is not the only one with a tendency to conflate want with need. I, too, have sat by and watched "want" slide lazily into "need" in our family conversations. We *need* to get AAA batteries before leaving on our road trip. We *need* to get some new throw pillows for the couch. I *need* a pair of navy shoes to wear with a new dress. Any close examination of our syntax would indicate that we are constantly in need. I know this not to be the case.

In an attempt to draw a bright line between want and need, I went to the (online) dictionary. Here is MerriamWebster.com on the noun "need": "1. A necessary duty or obligation; 2. A lack of something requisite, *desirable* or useful." Desirable?

And now, on the verb "to want": "1. To have a strong desire for; 2. To have *need* of." Need?

I am beginning to think it is not just our family that tends toward conflation here.

ལ∾

In his 1943 paper, "A Theory of Human Motivation," Abraham Maslow debuted his now famous Hierarchy of Needs, an iconic pyramid depicting how our higher order needs — self-actualization, self-esteem — rest on first having satisfied our more basic physiological and relational needs of food, safety, love and acceptance, and belonging. Though the framework has had its share of critics in psychological circles, I've always liked it. For me, Maslow's pyramid operates like a secret decoder key for human behavior, a reminder not to take other people's tension, stress, or anger personally. More often than not, the source of these emotions is a little bit of crumbling somewhere in the base of a person's pyramid—a sick parent, a divorce, a move.

Maslow came to mind as I was puzzling over this want/need question with Elliot, my almost-ten-year-old. Far more helpful than Merriam or Webster, Elliot offered the following response when I asked him how he would describe the difference between want and need: "Want is pretty much, like, optional. Need is, well, like not optional."

Maslow and Elliot have it right. It's hard to think about formulating a college savings plan when the electric company is

threatening to cut off the lights. The light bill *needs* to get paid
first. My middle school kid can't feel great about himself when
he is out of sorts with his friends. He first *needs* to feel a sense of
belonging among his peers. There is a requisite interdependency
and sense of progression built into the whole thing. Need gives
way to need, as want gives way to want, but satisfied need —
different from want — moves toward realized potential, a
fulfilled life, and ultimately, goodness toward others. In 1970,
Maslow added to his pyramid a topmost layer — Transcendence
— describing it as the state in which one reaches full actualization through the giving over of one's self to some higher goal
involving altruism or spirituality.

Continually satisfying our desires does not point us in this
direction. In fact, it is quite possible that it moves us in the opposite direction, as the Avett Brothers explain in their song "Ill with
Want":

> "I am sick with wanting.
> And it's evil how it's got me.
> And every day is worse than the one before.
> The more I have, the more I think,
> 'I'm almost where I need to be,
> if only I could get a little more.'"

If satisfied *need*, taken to the extreme, is actualization,
consistently satisfied *want*, the song seems to suggest, is
addiction.

ʚ৹

Desire is more than the anemic cousin of need. It is a singular-
ly powerful emotion, and no one understands that better than
those in charge of selling things to us. My family is enrolled in
a department store points program. In this ingenious strategy,
making purchases on specific dates gives you "triple points"
to be redeemed strategically on certain days. And — here's the

brilliant part — unused points eventually expire. Points equate to discounted dollars, and to remind you of this, the store sends you a note to tell you how many points (dollars) you have available, and also to alert you to their expiration date.

The first time we received one of these reminders during our year of no buying, my stomach lurched with anxiety. Fearful that we were leaving money on the table, I, chief guardian and enforcer of the no buying rules, panicked. I ran from the front hall clutching the reward certificate to find my husband to ask if we should make an exception and go shopping. The store had succeeded in creating in me a powerful mix of desire and obligation. To be a responsible steward of my points, I couldn't just let them disappear — good things might slip through my fingers.

Except, of course, there is no real money waiting for me at the store. To realize the value of the points, I had to first expend money on an item for which I did not have any intrinsic desire. No want existed before the store manufactured it in me. But once they did, my sense of desire didn't even have to be attached to a specific item to be activated. Through the point system they had created just enough urgency and hunger to get me in the door.

The magic of marketing is such that not only can it manufacture longing out of thin air, it can also take just a hint of interest and massage it into something more. Shortly before our no buying experiment started, my husband and I were considering a wooden trellis for our backyard. Clicking idly around on my computer, I followed a trail of links that led me to a website with discounted garden furniture, including a trellis of the type we had been discussing so—and here was my big mistake—I clicked on it.

In short order, that trellis, and others like it, found their way from around the Internet and onto my computer screen. Constantly. They were there when I checked my email, the weather, or the news. I found myself thinking more and more about a trellis until, when I looked out in my backyard, I could envision one where there was once only a notion. Since we were in the year-of-no buying, I did not click on anything again and the trellises (trelli?) began showing up with less frequency, gradually retreating to the various websites from whence they came.

Children hear the phrase "whet your appetite" as "wet your appetite"—which seems not entirely inaccurate, as though it might be a reference to our salivary glands. The actual phrase, however, means to sharpen one's taste for something, the "whet" referring to a whetstone, a device used to sharpen knives. This is how I think about what is happening with my stalker-trellis and the marketing scheme it represents. A raw lump of vague desire is gradually and deliberately honed by the messages all around us—beautiful pictures, low, low prices, convenient delivery, easy assembly. Without my even being aware, my appetite for a trellis is being slowly sharpened until this desire now takes the shape of a hook. Eventually, the tip will be so sharp that my want will snag. Were it not for the year of no buying, I would have eventually clicked again on the trellis, this time to buy it.

₭₮₱

Not all of our cravings have been manufactured or stoked by the forces of marketing. Human beings are obviously quite capable of genuine desire. It is the pang we feel when we come across something that delights and surprises us, and we therefore suddenly want to own it. It's the rush of emotion, unbidden, that my husband feels when he sees a Porsche drive past. Or when he walks into REI.

Children express genuine desire with great regularity and sincerity. On a recent trip to New York City we made our way to the NBC store at 30 Rockefeller Plaza. We'd been in the store no more than five minutes when Oliver and Foster came running up to us holding a mug decorated with *Parks and*

Recreation star Nick Offerman's mustachioed silhouette.
"Please," Foster begged, "it's Ron Swanson." The fervor
with which they made the case for the mug was impressive,
considering: (a) it was our year of no buying, (b) neither of them
drink coffee, and (c) it was a $17 mug with Nick Offerman's
face on it. The earnestness with which they explained why this
particular mug should be added to the collection of over 20 mugs
we already own could only have been born of real desire.

Genuine desire—different from manufactured or cultivated
want—deserves to be heeded, as it reveals truths about us or our
situations that have not necessarily been created or exagger-
ated by the forces of marketing. Our cravings are a part of the
mysterious algorithm that makes us who we are. The danger of
fully responding to this type of want, however, is that the way it
presents in our children—intense, fleeting—is true of our adult
desires too.

❧

Here was my mistake: in our consumer culture there is no bright
line between want and need. If there is any boundary between
them at all, it is porous. For years, the only functioning thermometer in our house was a digital ear thermometer that, for
some reason neither my husband or I could explain or fix, read
out in Celsius. We'd be woken in the middle of the night by the
cries of a feverish child, and in that drowsy and somewhat dread-
filled state that only a child in distress can produce, one of us
would take the temperature of the sick child huddled against our
chest, while the other would stumble around in the dark looking
for a smart phone so that we could convert the thermometer
reading to Fahrenheit. It was, in the words of our favorite sarcas-
tic 12-year-old friend, Max, "Genius."

Why, you wonder, did we not just take ourselves to the near-
est pharmacy and get a new thermometer? I have wondered this
many times. For starters, we only felt the need acutely at

two a.m. As soon as we had converted to Fahrenheit and had returned the sick child to bed, the more pressing purchase, the one
we would remember the following day, was Children's Tylenol.

But I also think, in the words of mothers and grandmothers
immemorial, we were just "making do" with our quirky thermometer. We lacked a perfect item, but we had jury-rigged a
good enough solution. And I think it is here that want finally
brushes up against need. Did we need a new thermometer? De-
batable. But here, at last, is the debate we should be having.

Our year of no buying forced us to dwell in this space, to
develop a tolerance for doing without. A few weeks into the year
we noticed that John's standard brown leather belt, the one he
wears to work almost every other day, was cracked and looking
shabby. In an attempt to forestall a purchase, Foster retrieved a
brown marker from his art set and colored in the cracks. I don't
think we were kidding ourselves to say the belt didn't look half
bad.

Eventually the marker will rub off, and at that time I suppose I will be willing to concede that we have approached something akin to need. John will need a new belt. In our privileged
lives, this lack of something daily or essential may be as close
as we will ever come to need. But it is still not need in the way
we understand food and shelter, or love and belonging, to be. A
brown leather belt is not critical to a fulfilled life.

Entire fortunes and a tremendous amount of human capital
are spent preventing us from remaining too long in this condition. Marketing professionals would have us lack for nothing;
eradicating the practice of "making do" in favor of buying early
and often. "Go ahead," they would tell John, "get that replacement belt. Do it now, while it's on sale. And maybe get an extra
one at half price while you're at it." To our ridiculous thermometer situation they would inquire in a solicitous tone, "Why do
that to yourselves?"

Why indeed? It's hard to come up with a defense for

restraint. The best most of us can do is give a weak nod to environmental concerns—why add another digital thermometer to the landfill? But in truth, we know that our new thermometer has already been made, shipped, and stocked at our local pharmacy. As have 100,000 more like it. We're already too late. If we don't buy it, someone else will.

The case for attending to, and ultimately fulfilling our desires is all around us. It's omnipresent and incessant and drowns out most everything else. But if we listen only to this siren song, we will miss the good stuff of the pyramid: relationship and love, self-efficacy and change. Maslow's list of needs isn't just psychological formulation; it is a recipe for a meaningful life. It falls to us to resurrect the case for our real needs; to listen for them, to draw the conclusion anew for ourselves. In the dark of my sick child's bedroom, what he needs—what we *both* need—is to simply hold tight to one another while we wait for the fever to pass.

ALL CONSUMING

In the last week of 2017, on a trip to New Jersey to visit my sister, John's wallet was stolen during the flight, a fact that seemed improbable to the point of being untrue. After we landed, he and the flight attendants spent 20 minutes searching under seat cushions and through the trash, certain he must have dropped it somewhere in flight. When he finally walked off the jetway, still walletless, we were forced to move on from the lost-or-stolen question to face the fact that the wallet was, in any case, gone. We cancelled our joint credit card and his work credit card. What we forgot, however, is that he had two other cards in that wallet, an older joint credit card that we rarely used, and a department store card.

In early March we began receiving emails from our bank and the department store inquiring about unusual charges on these cards up and down the Eastern Seaboard: $374 at a CVS outside of Washington D.C., $486 at a Nordstrom in Cherry Hill, New Jersey, and $500-and-change at a store called Dudes in Philadelphia. This last one was the clincher – neither of us had ever set foot in a Dudes.

The discovery of the fraud on our card was a relief. John's wallet had indeed been stolen. No one was happier to hear this than John, who prides himself on a surplus of basic common sense and competency. Shortly after we left the airport in the rental car that I, still in possession of my license, was driving, he turned to me and said, "How did I lose my wallet? I can't believe I'm *that* guy." The murky circumstances surrounding the wallet's disappearance left him blaming himself rather than raging at a potential thief. Months later, the news that someone was on a spending spree with his stolen wallet was an absolution. He wasn't *that* guy, after all.

I had to laugh as this seemed to be some kind of cosmic joke. Here we had been studiously refraining from buying anything for a full three months, and there was our alter ego on the East Coast making up for every last bit of our restraint. It was as though we had a karmic shopping credit destined to be spent one way or another.

You might assume that I took a kind of vicarious joy in the thief's actions. That in some way it felt right that at least one person was out there buying a new spring wardrobe—especially since, according to the credit card company, neither we nor the thief were apparently going to have to pay for it. But the truth is, I didn't have a pent-up purchasing need in search of release. In fact, I hadn't missed shopping at all. I am at best a mediocre shopper. I have no particular aversion to it, but I have neither the drive of a bargain hunter nor the intuition of a stylist. I rest somewhere uncomfortably between the two—a mixture which frequently results in the purchase of cheap and trendy clothes from discount stores that fail to satisfy on either count. More often than not, when I find the perfect item of clothing at full price, I balk at the amount and walk away.

In the process of not shopping, I discovered a second thing I dislike about it: stores are a gateway to unplanned acquisition. This, I have since been informed, is an actual phenomenon known as the "Target Effect," referring to the Minneapolis-based chain department store—also ironically inferring the opposite of the word's real meaning. You enter Target intending to pick up a Lego set for the birthday party your child will be attending. En route to the store, you catch a glimpse of your Saturday-morning self in the rearview mirror and think, "Wow, could I benefit from some mascara." Unbeknownst to your conscious mind, you've now given yourself permission to head over to Cosmetics, which involves a swing through the Dollar Spot, which is adjacent to Housewares. And somehow, before you really know what has happened, you are in the checkout line holding two scented candles, a water bottle, mascara, eyeliner, the Lego set, and an extra-large carton of Goldfish crackers. Things have gone decidedly off-target.

In my dream world, our extended shopping sabbatical will leave me changed. I will think twice before going to the store to begin with, but once there I will look for and purchase just what I came to get. I will refrain from the impulse buy—the colorful beach bag hanging on the aisle end-cap. I will know and remember that there is a blue and white beach bag from last year in our downstairs closet that works just fine. I will walk in, get the Lego set, pay for it, and get out. I will shop with a sense of purpose and intentionality. I will be the opposite of our East Coast thief. I will not buy simply because I can.

❧

That we buy largely to communicate we have the capacity to is not a new idea. In 1899, Norwegian-American economist Thorstein Veblen coined the term "conspicuous consumption" to refer to the purchasing of unnecessary, luxury items by what he termed "the leisure class," those able to reside at a distance from the hard, manual labor of production. Veblen, writing at the end of the first Gilded Age, had spent a lifetime observing the behavior of the rich. The leisure class was not just buying excess goods, he noted, but buying unnecessarily expensive basic items—and in so doing, conflating beauty and utility in a way that confounded traditional economics. When presented with two equally serviceable spoons, Veblen points out, traditional economic theory suggests that the consumer's choice should be the cheaper, machine-made spoon that costs less to make and has a higher degree of per-item perfection. In economic terms, this choice would be both the rational and efficient one. The wealthy, he observed, were more likely to purchase a hand-wrought, silver spoon that costs more to make (and therefore buy) and yet provides equal value to the user. So why the more expensive spoon?

The silver spoon, Veblen explains, is an honorific. Its hand-made beauty, weight, and overall aesthetic has been deemed valuable by a group of people who, privileged by their distance from labor, did not have to value efficiencies. Their judgments about taste gradually seeped into the larger culture and mixed with our understanding of beauty. One lasting effect of the conspicuous consumption by the leisure class according to Veblen is that we buy expensive things precisely because they are expensive, and therefore, we believe, beautiful.

The problem persists. Over a decade ago, our entire family converted to the exclusive use of Apple products. My husband led the charge on this decision, making a well-founded argument about superior performance. After my ancient PC crashed for the sixth time in two days, I gave in. We are now all Apple, all the time. We each own an iPhone and there are two iPads in operation at our house. John's office runs on Macs, and I am writing this manuscript on a MacBook Pro. Since making the switch, I haven't looked back.

Apple products are an interesting Veblen case study. They are arguably better performers at many basic computing, and even non-computing (think cameras and phones) tasks. Throw in the question of innovation, and it seems that one could make a real argument for efficiency and value in our choice to consume them. On the other hand, what if Apple products are simply honorifics? What if by virtue of their gorgeous design and higher price point we have endowed them with a weighted value when they perform only marginally better, if at all, than their less expensive counterparts? I know many people who believe this; I could call any one of them on their Samsung Galaxy and get an ardent defense of just this idea.

The notion that Apple products have more value as status symbols than actual computing machines is one I dare not utter aloud in my house. It's not that we haven't considered other brands, but a switch would upset an entire eco-system of technology and connection around which much of our life operates. If one of us were to depart the world of Apple, calendars would not sync, messages would fail to be received, and general havoc would ensue.

Technology has calcified and made explicit the very tendencies Veblen was writing about. In his day, leisure class preferences were, like most trends, implicit albeit powerful. When it comes to the technology of today, conspicuous consumption inadvertently creates its own mandate, having become tangled up with issues of utility and connection in new and complicated ways. Put bluntly, it is harder and harder to back down from a particular level of consumption. Alas, Veblen saw this coming too: "When the individual has once formed the habit of seeking expression in a given line of honorific expenditure," he writes, "...it is with extreme reluctance that such an habitual expenditure is given up."

કેબ્જ

Even after the credit card fiasco was resolved, I continued to think from time to time about our thief. Had he (the purchases at Dudes prompting my use of the male pronoun here) consumed out of distraction and capacity, like my Target-shopping self, or had he, like Veblen's leisure class, wanted to communicate something about himself through the things he bought?

To understand consuming in only these terms doesn't allow

for a very charitable read on our thief, or extrapolating out, on the whole of humanity. Ascribing either motivation to our consumption paints us as ignorant and striving, a mass of bored consumers carried along in the currents of marketing or under the spell of celebrity influencers.

My friend Sarah is a social worker with a high empathy set point. Like Veblen, she acknowledges that our things are meant to serve as proxy, but she's more generous in her suggestion of what they are proxy for. We consume, she believes, not simply out of boredom or to put our wealth on display, but as an extension of ourselves as caretakers and providers. After learning about our no buying experiment, she texted me with reservations about buying a $250 pair of basketball shoes for her high school player. "What about those times when buying is about your role performance as a mother?" she asked, after admitting to making the purchase. There are times when our consumption might be less about communicating status and instead, a way of indicating that we believe in our children or spouse, that we want them to succeed in their endeavors, and that we love them. This is the hunch Sarah has.

I'd like to sit Veblen down to tea to talk about this. (Obviously, I'd get out the good spoons.) If industrialization and an abundance of wealth allowed consumption to function as proxy for leisure and status, at what point did consumption become a proxy for care? Is it only lately, since we find ourselves with both so little time and so much access to so many things? Or has it always been thus? And when, if ever, is this kind of consumption okay?

The problem is that consuming thoughtfully doesn't necessarily equate to thoughtful consumption. Which is to say that even when we buy something for another as an action of care and connection, we are still consuming. Even, perhaps especially, in these scenarios, we are acquiring and accumulating outside the space of real need. And when we send the signal, to our children in particular, that the quantity and quality of their goods somehow indicates how well they are loved, conspicuous consumption takes on new meaning. It moves into dangerous territory past our boredom and ego and straight to our very humanity. Our capacity for care and connection becomes bound up in what we buy.

Our culture's excessive consumption is not simply conspicuous or complex, it is confused. I am no exception. At my best, I buy to care for others, or as a form of authentic self-expression. But I also consume to communicate something about my own competency; my value somehow implied in the goods I bring home. I am most wont to shop when bored and vulnerable to distraction. This lack of clarity works to the benefit of the seller. Clicking "Buy Now" gives me a vague sense of having accomplished something, though I'd be hard-pressed to say exactly what. As with our thief, I may never know the real motivation behind my purchases. The longer I fail to ask the question, the more and more I consume.

MINE TO CHOOSE

In an essay in the October 2018 issue of *The New York Times Magazine*, author Jason Diamond examines his Saturday ritual of eating a bialy for breakfast. Defending a quirky bit of personal routine, he uses the piece to explore the problem of excessive choice. "In a time where you can stream any song, order any widget from Amazon or get every bit of bad news in real time," writes Diamond, "it's pleasurable and rare not to have choices. You pick a bialy and that's what you get."

Opening with a brunch-induced panic attack, his essay is both a paean to an oft-overlooked breakfast food and a meditation on the very questions of choice, want, and need that have obsessed me of late. Between my interest in these topics and my general love of eating, I was set up to enjoy the piece thoroughly, and would have were it not for the cover of the magazine.

The cover of the October 2018 issue features a close-up photo of a Yemini mother in full burka, holding her naked, starving child. We are spared no detail of the child's condition; distended belly, limp wrinkles of mocha skin where a chubby baby butt should be, matchstick thin wrists and legs, and a face in which the eyes and teeth are dominant as the rest of the features sink in, skull-like, behind them. The child's oversized eyes are downcast, gazing with confusion at the gauzy bandage encircling its tiny wrist. The photograph works on the viewer the way all the most devastating photographs do: you want to turn away and yet you can't stop taking it in.

On an average week, one in which the cover story was less dire, Diamond's bialy piece would have been right at home in a magazine that includes ads for Manhattan condos with discreet taglines like "Units Starting at $8M." Behind a cover featuring a starving child, however, the essay reads differently. At best, Diamond's more philosophical ruminations evaporate into relative meaninglessness, and the work instead becomes a comic fluff piece featuring a bit of New York agita. Poor guy! So overwhelmed by choices! At worst, he reads like an oblivious American, lamenting an excess of both food and choice, blissfully ignorant of the dire situation that resulted in the starving child on the cover.

While unfortunate timing for Diamond, who likely had no say in the choice of cover, the juxtaposition of the starving child with the bialy essay brought two ideas into sharp relief for me. First, there is a daily Alice in Wonderland phenomenon at play, in which my personal wants and needs (such as they are) take on giant proportions in the context of my life, and then suddenly, when held up against the pain of the larger world, shrink into nothingness. Can it be that I truly experience longing, or the audacity to have preferences, when I have so much relative to so many? And once having understood my own desires as so very minor or pesky in the scheme of the world, how do I attend to them appropriately? When, if ever, are they even worthy of attention?

Second, the proximity of the Diamond piece to the Yemeni child forced me to ask how is it that too much choice has become burdensome? How can this be possible when so many people have no choice at all? On the cover, a mother with no options. In light of her plight, and the agony of the child in her arms, how can choice ever be viewed as anything other than a luxury? What were the limited choices that created this untenable situation in the first place? At this point, what few choices remain?

☙❧

The literature on choice has been prolific in the last few years. With an increase in our options comes an increase in our thinking about our options. "Most modern Americans live in a bountiful world. While we don't get to do and have everything we want, no other people on earth have ever had such control over their lives, such material abundance, and such freedom of choice," observes Barry Schwartz whose book, *The Paradox of Choice,* names exactly how this trend has played out for us.

The general consensus of the research is as follows: when it comes to choice, human beings reach a moment at which additional options become more harmful than beneficial. This point, research suggests, is the moment at which our choices become so numerous that we can no longer make them wisely and with full freedom. Overloaded by options and information on how to choose among those options, we become "pickers" – people reflexively responding to what's before us, and not "choosers" – people thoughtfully considering their options. When we are not free to make our decisions carefully, in a way that reflects our real wants and needs, we are less likely to be happy with them, and more likely to experience depression and regret. Dubbed "choice overload," this phenomenon runs rampant in today's society.

The literature documents the ways in which the experience of choice overload is the result of cognitive processes, but I want to argue that it is the result of some moral dissonance as well. We're not just exhausted by the prospect of constantly working through a complex set of decisions about everything from our retirement plans to our razors, we're discouraged by the sense that it ultimately may not be possible to choose well – to make choices with implications that are kind to our fellow human beings or to the earth. In this information-saturated time, even the simplest decisions have a gotcha feel.

To wit: my growing family is constantly running out of
bread, peanut butter, bananas, and milk. I'm in the grocery store
a lot. To grocery shop in my town is to ask yourself whether you
want to save money and spend wisely at Food-4-Less or Aldi,
care for your health and the environment by shopping at Whole
Foods, encourage local employment by heading to Valli Produce
or Jewel Osco, or support farm-to-table eating and our local
growers at the farmers' market. Each decision has an inverse
implication – buying from big agriculture, practicing cultural
elitism. When I stand in the produce section of whatever store
I have selected on a given day, a banana is rarely ever just a
banana.

ॐॐॐ

Concurrent with the rise of choice overload is a growth in "choice
architects," the people in charge of creating the structures into
which we make our choices. Although their work sounds like the
province of marketing, choice architects are at work everywhere;
for instance, investment managers who sum up the pros and
cons of mutual funds to help simplify the options and guide the
selection process for their clients.

Anyone who has ever parented or taught small children is
a practicing choice architect. Would you like carrots or celery
sticks with your lunch? Which hat are you going to wear today?
Assumptions are embedded and lines are drawn: you, child, will
be wearing a hat. Such is the power of the choice architect. In
their recent book *Nudge*, economists Richard Thaler and Cass
Sunstein acknowledge this power, and propose what a responsible way of deploying it, one they deem "libertarian paternalism"
– freedom of choice accompanied by select information or an
incentive which functions as a nudge in the right direction.

In endorsing this approach, Thaler and Sunstein attempt
to address a central tension at work in many choice scenarios:
the relative value of personal freedom versus the commitment

to a larger public good, a tension that seems to become more pronounced with each passing day. Interesting though it is, like much of the literature on choice, their analysis involves only the choice architect and the chooser. It does not have much to offer the choiceless.

∝୧୨∝

The vexing problem is this: we cannot reallocate the resource of choice. I can cut down on the number of choices I make, and I can make the choices I somehow perceive as most responsible, but by doing so, I cannot guarantee more choice for others. Try as I might, I cannot directly provide more options to that Yemini mother. Some relief or resources, perhaps. But choice, no.

As a person of privilege in possession of real options, it then falls to me to make ethical decisions that, however feebly, attempt to acknowledge our interconnectedness. I can strive, as Ghandi suggests, to live simply so that others may simply live. But in this complex and global time, it is hard to trace that thread. I struggle to see how the choices made about my own life will ultimately impact the planet, or affect the lives of those most desperately in need. It's a fact I must take on faith.

Depending on your capacity for faith, it is possible to become paralyzed here. And this brings us back to Diamond and his bialy. "I've learned that all these wants, the constant stream of choices that is daily life, crowd my brain. I'm wasting precious time by busying myself with pointless deciding." Ultimately, he writes, "I should focus on the moment at hand: the bialy, the butter, the easy choice." This call for simplicity and presence – two responses possible in almost any situation – is perhaps a starting place.

A year of no buying is, by definition, a year of less choice. One major decision that wipes a lot of other decisions off the board. By removing even a fraction of the choices we faced, we made incrementally more room for the things that matter. The year has been, in Diamond's words, a chance to focus on the moment at hand. This simplifying and being present, it will not end starvation or reverse climate change. But, I am hopeful, it is a nudge in the right direction.

OH CRAP

My husband's stepmother was 15 when she answered an ad in a magazine and received a German pen pal. Angelika in Koln, Germany, and Linda in Detroit, Michigan, wrote to each other faithfully throughout their adolescence. Upon reaching adulthood, they upgraded their epistolary friendship to an in-person one, and ultimately an intergenerational one. When I first met John, his parents were hosting Angelika's son, Carsten, during his high school year abroad.

This September, the Germans, as they are known affectionately to our family, were scheduled to fly into Chicago before setting off for Linda the following day. We had promised to host them during their Chicago overnight, offering a "real American" cookout complete with hot dogs, hamburgers, potato chips, and a conspicuous lack of vegetables. My children were thrilled.

Alas, The Germans missed their flight. The whole thing involved a passport left at home and a rebooked flight out of Amsterdam. The Germans felt terrible. There was some initial talk about trying to reschedule for the following night, when they would arrive on a new flight, but here, I will admit, I was resistant; the next day was my birthday, and we had family plans.

September is also an unforgiving month where the schedule is concerned. Each day is crammed with approximately 16 events (curriculum night, soccer game, play rehearsal). When an event is scratched from the calendar, there is no making it up. There is only moving on.

Two September weeks sped by and before I knew it the Germans were back. John agreed to host them for lunch and made some gentle inquiries about my joining them. I flatly refused, pointing to a wall calendar so heavily notated it was practically illegible. He set off to meet them alone.

As per September, I was out for an evening meeting that night. Returning around eight, I was surprised to see John and the boys still seated at the kitchen table. The dishes were in various stages of being cleared, and the rest of the table was littered with wrapping paper and a smattering of colorful objects. My boys were laughing. The teakettle whistled in the background.

I put down my bag and stepped closer to take in the scene. It turns out the Germans had brought gifts – lots of them – and had given them to John to pass along to us. There were bags of German gummy candies, hand-woven placemats in fantastic bright and navy shades of blue (Helmut, Angelika's husband, has a loom), and a board game for the boys. Remembering it was my birthday, Helmut had woven mittens and a wooly headband for me. For John, there was a Koln football team t-shirt. And the *piéce de résistance* (and also the reason for the whistling tea kettle), they had brought us Mr. Tea... a little pliable figure who separates at the waist so you can fill his pants with loose tea leaves and hang him, hot tub style, from the edge of your teacup to steep your tea. They had also provided the loose tea, mango-flavored, just in case we didn't have any on hand. When I walked in, Oliver had the kettle on, preparing to give Mr. Tea a go.

And now, a moment of honesty. Upon surveying the scene, my first thought was, "Crap!" (an exclamation, not a description, though both work), "What are we going to do with all of this stuff?" We already have a wand apparatus designed to hold loose tea, and frankly, we're a teabag family. We aren't hurting for placemats either.

Until this moment, standing before the bounty on my kitchen table, I don't think I understood the shift that been occurring in me. If, in the face of all this generosity, "crap" was the only response I could muster, I had become a little warped. A little lost.

❧

There is another night each year when a load of gifts is disgorged onto our kitchen table. It is the night my husband returns from his annual industry conference bearing a tote bag full of conference swag. When my boys were small, the unpacking and distribution of the swag ranked up there with Christmas morning and their birthdays. To this day, my jaded teenagers will still gather round when John unloads the loot.

My husband does not work in a cutting-edge industry. He does not return with the latest toys, tech, or high-end beauty products. The corporate gifts that make up his swag reflect the workaday nature of his business: post-its, plastic letter openers, beer koozies, squishy stress balls, and packages of M&Ms bearing various company logos. We've gotten water bottles, umbrellas and even, one memorable year, a selfie-stick which became a sword in the hands of my seven-year-old. (Were no parents involved in the swag selection?) Still, other companies have gone the humorous route, distributing little glasses encouraging you to "take a shot" on them, or a spray bottle of air freshener promising you'll "never be Number 2" with their company.

I hate swag.

If you asked my children, they would tell you this hatred was yet another manifestation of my reflexive anti-stuff stance. That I am pretty much a party pooper of the first magnitude. Had you asked *me*, however, I would have told you it was actually this: that after everyone sorts through the swag to claim their preferred item, they run off and leave the rest of the junk in a pile on the kitchen table, never to be revisited again.

Each year this pile creates a conundrum for me. My first impulse is always to sweep the entire mess into a garbage bag and take it directly to the curb. But year after year, the little Depression-era grandmother perched on my shoulder prevents me from doing so. Just as I reach for a tiny logo-adorned plastic tape measure containing only enough tape to measure maybe two feet, I hear a voice. "Wait," she cautions, "do we have a tape measure? I mean, do we even know where our rulers are? What if someone's math homework requires measuring in units of inches?" On my other shoulder sits the eco-fairy. Unlike the angel and devil, these two never fight. The eco-fairy agrees with everything grandma says, and then points out how much waste I'd be adding to the landfill if I pitched these things. So it is that the crap stays.

Swag has no natural home in our homes. Sure, maybe the office supplies can be stuffed in a desk drawer, or the water bottle added to an already massive collection, but in my house there is no display cabinet for shot glasses, no self-evident selfie stick storage. Each year the swag hangs around for months, cluttering desktops and filling junk drawers, adding to the flotsam and jetsam of our common living space.

That swag does not insert easily into our daily lives is not surprising, These gifts were never intended specifically for us. In her book *Crap: A History of Cheap Stuff in America*, author Wendy Woloson describes the origins of corporate gifting. Intended to curry favor with potential customers rather than reward purchasing, these "advertising specialties" – leatherbound diaries, glass paperweights imprinted with company insignias – constituted the first effort by marketers to insinuate themselves in our homes. "The very existence of the advertising specialty, to say nothing of its veritable overnight success," she notes, "was a testament to the ability of marketing professionals to blur the public and private spheres, the commercial and the personal." Wildly successful with retail customers, corporate gifts then made their way to the upper echelons of Corporate America where, at the executive level, fancy pens and cocktail sets became a means of cementing what Woloson describes as "pseudo-personal intimacies" among the top brass.

Despite a general acknowledgement of its insincerity, corporate gifting has taken root and become an expected part of modern business transactions. As of 2015, the manufacturing, importing and distribution of swag constituted a $20.8 trillion industry. Slightly more disturbing is the deleterious effect swag has had on our overall cultural practice of gift giving. The pervasiveness of swag, Woloson suggests, has made it "harder to distinguish gifts from commodities and, hence to determine what their exchange actually means." These advertising tactics, she explains, exploit the fact that no gift is without a sense of some obligation on the part of the receiver. "Advertising specialties, like 'regular' gifts, created debts and obligations, but repayment was to be made through commercial mechanisms." The quid pro quo of swag turns out to be more consumption. And when we exchange gifts intending to monetize our relationships rather than celebrate them, we corrupt the basic human impulse to give and receive.

Perhaps most problematic, she observes, is the fact that swag solidifies the unique identity of the giver over and above the receiver and reinforces the receiver as consumer. Whereas a gift would typically be made special by personalizing it for the receiver with a monogram or other inscription, swag perverts this relationship. It comes bearing the insignia of the corporate gifter, marked with the logo of the company. "In this way," Woloson observes, "advertising specialties took Emerson's dictum that the only true gift 'is a portion of thyself' to its logical market-driven end: the gift bore the markings of the business's identity, while the recipient was just another interchangeable customer."

❧

The teakettle continued to shriek as I stood there looking from the German gifts to my smiling boys and back again. Moving toward the table, I slid on my handmade mittens and took a seat next to John, who was already wearing his new t-shirt over his work shirt. Elliot passed me the gummies as Oliver showed off Mr. Tea lounging in a steaming mug of hot water. Sitting around that joyful table, it occurred to me that the Germans had remembered my birthday and worried over whether we would have loose tea. When making our placemats, Helmut had taken into account the color of our kitchen. These gifts were, most specifically, for us.

Suddenly, I wished I could thank them in person.

My family's life is not only filled with stuff. It is just filled, period. And there are times when we fill it to such a point that spontancity and serendipity are completely out of the question. This was the situation in which we found ourselves this September. Missed flight? No time to see our friends, or to borrow a term from another era, *receive* them in our home. It's all tied up together. We have too much. We move too fast. The deep and sustained rhythm of a pen pal relationship has no place in modern life.

Woloson arrives at the same conclusion. At the end of her book, in an attempt to summarize the whole of our uniquely American fascination with meaningless things – swag, collectibles, unnecessary gadgets – she can infer but one thing. The root of the problem does not lie with the motives of the marketers or in the prevalence of the objects. Swag points not to a corruption in our gift giving, but instead a cheapening of our very character, the result of lifetimes spent immersed in consumer culture. We value worthless crap because, over time, we ourselves have, in Woloson's words, "become crappy." With swag, she posits, and the thousands of other meaningless items that flow through our lives, we are getting precisely what we deserve.

DIRTY HANDS

The guy in front of me is making awkward small talk, wiping his moist hands down the front of his jeans. Small talk is common at the dump, where publicly sorting your trash leaves you exposed and looking to distract. "When I was a kid," he is saying to all of us and no one in particular as he piles empties on a table, the glass bottles clinking together, "we used to pull up, dump all our trash in a mound, get back in the car and wait for the bears to come." With that pronouncement, he looks around once more – maybe for bears – dusts his hands together a final time as if to be rid of the whole experience and climbs back in his car.

We are standing in the municipal dump in the mountain town where, like my mother before me, and her mother before her, I retreat each summer with my family. The phenomenon of bears at the dump, however, ended with my mother's childhood. By the time my sister and I were children, the dump had begun to clean itself up, so to speak. "No more bears at the dump these days," my grandfather announced during one of our summer visits after my mom expressed a desire to check. "Better for us, and better for the bears."

Ridding the dump of bears was not its only move toward modernization. The sign out on the road leading to the dump now reads "Inlet Transfer Station," though everyone still calls it the dump. Inside, rather than pulling up and dropping bags of trash in a communal refuse pile, well-trained residents get out of their cars with their garbage bags and containers of recyclables to be separated into various categories: plastic, aluminum, glass, paper (glossy and cardstock included), and corrugated card-board. Despite all this sorting, it is unclear to me what exactly is being "transferred," and where. I can see why, at least among the old-timers in my family, the name has failed to stick.

I look forward to our trip to the mountains every summer. For starters, it is an opportunity to unplug and tune out from the barrage of email, text, news briefs, and phone calls that make for the staccato rhythm of our daily life. In the mountains, where there is still no cell signal and the Wi-Fi is spotty, days have a slow, soothing rhythm all their own. There are no interruptions; we move quietly and intentionally from one activity to the next. In fact, by the standard of our regular life, much of what we do – reading, napping, cooking – would barely register as activity at all. The downside, as my preteen and teenage boys would be quick to tell you, is boredom. Bereft of their screens, it always takes them a cranky day or two to adjust to the pace. Without digital distractions, my boys are left to reckon with themselves, the limits of their abilities, and their sense of possibilities.

It is not just children who require an adjustment period. Adults removed from their urban habitat have to do a little reck-oning of their own. For me, this reckoning happens at the dump. Not only is there no cell signal where we stay, but neither is there garbage pick-up. Taking out the trash involves loading bags of garbage into the trunk of your car and hauling them to the local dump. So it is that those three weeks in upstate New York are the only time in my life when I am forced to come face to face with the fate of an item once I am through with it – a process that is unsettling, to say the least.

❧

I grew up in Chicago, a town with a liberal garbage policy, and in a family that threw its used batteries directly in the trash. For most of my life, the garbage can has signified the end of my relationship with a discarded item. Lift lid, insert item, all done. My husband, on the other hand, has lived in towns that make you tag and pay for your garbage per bag. In college he had a summer internship with the National Recycling Coalition. Not surprisingly, he's given a little more thought to the matter of where things end up.

Occasionally, this has been a point of tension in our marriage. In our early city-dwelling years, he'd come home to find me cramming, say, a broken office chair into our city-issued can and shake his head in disbelief. I tried to explain to him that in Chicago, were I to stuff a small child in the trash, the can would be returned empty, no questions asked. Despite these assurances, he would still get nervous when I would pull the can out to the alley, lid ajar, two-by-fours or some such thing protruding. The next morning when we would find the can empty and waiting, I believe he was equal parts awed and disgusted.

Equal parts awed and disgusted may also be an apt description of my reaction to our mountain dump. A trip to the dump overwhelms the senses, though not in a wholly unpleasant way. Summer in the mountains is perpetually wet. Constant moisture mixed with summer heat draws out the sweet, rotting smell particular to garbage en masse. On hot days the smell veers toward stink, but on an average mountain day, I'd go with pungent. Its all-encompassing power takes me by surprise whenever I drive in.

The omnipresence of the smell is rivaled only by the sheer scale of the garbage, glorious in its colorful magnitude. The dump's primary sorting area is a warehouse, open floor to ceiling, and easily two stories high. After dumping bulging bags of food waste in the designated area, residents pull out their recycling containers and proceed to put their recyclables on the appropriate table, which serves only as an initial stop for the item in question. Shortly after the items are placed there, the lady who staffs the dump – we'll call her Terri – comes along and tosses the bottles and cans into large piles located just beyond them, a kind of secondary sorting involving frequent loud crashes and the breaking of glass. Hers has always struck me as a strangely satisfying job.

The gigantic piles of recyclables that mount up behind the sorting tables form a crude approximation of the real mountain range, just beyond the perimeter of the dump. Out there, in the real mountains, tent campers buy and use plastic five-gallon containers of water for their campsites. Inexplicably, despite the potable well water available from the tap in most lake houses, many other vacationers do the same. Once discarded, the ghostly white water containers eventually pile up into huge cascading mounds behind the dump's plastics table. As the mounds of plastic get unmanageable, Terri gets in her forklift and drives it fearlessly into the towering heap. I have never stuck around long enough to see what happens next.

❧❧

According to the Trash Pirates, a movement of young people cleaning up the mess left in the wake of large music festivals, there's such a thing as a "trash moment" – a single instant in which one understands the vastness of the waste we produce. "Your first experience of the mass , whether it's loading dumpsters onto a trailer, or driving out to the event grounds when everyone is gone and it's a sea of trash, is an existential crisis," says Sophia Nielsen to *The New York Times*, as she sews the bones of a greasy spent chicken wing onto her shirt outside the Joshua Tree Music Festival. Nielsen is a Trash Pirate. Like normal twenty-somethings, she and her cohorts attend these festivals. But unlike their peers, they stick around to pick up what's been

left behind. The discarded chicken wing on her shirt? Aware-
ness-raising.

Music festivals are an exercise in enormity of scale: thousands of bodies, tens of thousands of tattoos, millions of paper
wrist bands sprinkled like confetti over the grass, unimagin-
ably long rows of port-a-potties, and the even longer lines of
people waiting for their turn to go. (Some kinds of waste can't
be ignored.) I have been to enough festivals to catch the high
that results from a mass of humanity set to music. I love them.
But aside from feeling moderately distressed by the sickening
number of plastic bottles overflowing their designated recycling
containers, I have chosen to refrain from contemplating what is
left in our wake after we all go home.

The Trash Pirates don't contemplate. They clean. And they
don't just clean – they sort and sift, reuse and repurpose. They
make their way slowly across festival lawns, picking up hundreds
of thousands of individual cigarette butts, sending them off to be
compressed into pallets. They sort through and compost the food
scraps of Burning Man campers who are disinclined to do so
for themselves. They get doused in "garbage juice" as they work
Coachella, heaving bags of wet waste into trucks. Perhaps, most
miraculously, they do all this with joy; making art with the trash,
steampunk style, and wearing it while singing and dancing their
way through the festivals, interacting with concertgoers, and
gently drawing people's attention toward the amassing detritus.
This is not spot cleaning; the Pirates are after culture change.
"We are trying to alter the cultural norms of a throwaway society," one of them explains to the reporter, "We are trying to
teach them that there's no 'away.'"

❧

During most of my life, two frustrated locals in reflective vests
staffed our mountain dump. It was clear that they could not get

over the gross ignorance and basic incompetence of the summer tourist population (likely for good reason). For years, I thought that the general sense of shame I felt during my visits to the dump was a byproduct of being assumed an idiot, just by driving onto the premises with out-of-state plates. Last year, the two dump veterans were replaced by the aforementioned Terri, a professional and cheerful woman in her forties, who is only too glad to help answer questions and join in the sorting of trash.

Despite the change in tone, each time I visit the dump, I leave feeling vaguely icky. Not I-didn't-fully-rinse-out-the-jar-of-peanut-butter-and-now-it's-on-my-hands icky, but deeply uncomfortable. Standing in the dump brings me face to face with two inescapable and troublesome realities: (1) I am constantly contributing to an already unmanageable amount of waste, and (2) for most of the year, it is possible for me to ignore this fact and let other people deal with it, literally never getting my hands dirty.

Our little mountain town has a year-round population of 310 – a population that grows maybe tenfold during The Season. The garbage mountains I see during my twice-weekly trips to the dump are the product of a mere 3,000 of us. There are currently approximately eight billion people on earth.

↝↜

In 1993, I travelled to Egypt with my college. Between excursions to mosques and the tombs of Pharaohs, our group made a brief stop in Manshiyat Nasser – Cairo's Garbage City – nestled in the heart of the booming metropolis. We had come to Garbage City in search of Coptic Christians, a persecuted religious minority struggling to survive in predominantly Muslim Egypt. For centuries, a group of Copts, called the Zabbaleen, have served as Cairo's garbage collectors, taking the waste of some 20 million people in the metropolitan area, and effectively and efficiently disposing of much of it. With a 90% recycling or reuse rate, the Copts operate at four-times the efficiency of most Western recycling companies.

Despite the valuable service they offer to the larger community, Manshiyat Nasser is one of Cairo's poorest neighborhoods, lacking a sewer system, electricity, and other basic infrastructure. In Garbage City, trash lines the streets and the doorways of buildings, fills the rooms of people's homes, resulting in a strange mix of grime, stink, and riotous color that at once is aesthetically appealing and entirely off-putting. While there, our group visited an organization for women who salvage the city's textiles, shredding them into rags and weaving them into rugs. To see their work we had to wind our way to a back room of a local house, moving through dim narrow passageways filled with teetering piles of filthy fabric. When we arrived at the space where their wares were on display, we saw that, in anticipation of our visit, the women had woven the name of our college into some of the rugs.

The contrast of the name of our elite private college stitched into Cairo's trash was not lost on us. At the end of the visit, purchased rugs in hand, we boarded the tour bus on which we'd come and sat quietly as it bumped and wove its way through the streets of Garbage City and out into the Cairo traffic. Though no one wanted to say it, we were relieved to be driving away from the stench and chaos, grateful that garbage collection was not our lot in life.

In 2003, almost a decade after I visited Garbage City, officials in Cairo decided to privatize garbage collection, forcing the Coptic garbage collectors and their ramshackle trucks to compete with the technology of modern waste management corporations. As if this change were not stressful enough on the Zabbaleen, around this same time, a swine flu scare prompted officials to slaughter every hog in Cairo, including the pigs who lived in Garbage City methodically eating up Cairo's organic waste.

Fattened on the scraps of a city, the hogs had also been a source of income for the garbage collectors, who sold them to shops and restaurants for meat. This double blow means that today, waste management is proving to be difficult business for the residents of Garbage City.

⚚

Last summer, my uncle came by with his trailer so we could take some larger items to the dump. As we loaded in a plastic lawn chair and an outdated TV, it occurred to me that I had never before tried to throw out non-perishable or non-recyclable items of any significant size at the dump. In Chicago, I knew just what to do with these things; put them in a garbage can and – poof – they would disappear. In the mountains, I was forced to contemplate the specific next steps for the items I wished to dispose of. With no small degree of panic, I realized I didn't know what they were.

The TV turned out to be no problem. In one corner of the dump was a small hill of broken electronics that had failed to catch my attention during previous visits. Broken-screen TVs and various outdated computer components – modems, keyboards – formed a haphazard pile. Since electronics are one of the items covered in the Transfer Station brochure, I was certain something productive was going to happen with this pile. As we dropped the TV onto the mound, it was still possible for me to believe that there was a future in which it would be dismembered, recycled, repurposed... .

The plastic lawn chair was a different story. Turning to Terri, I held up the chair and inquired hopefully, "Plastics?"

"Nope," said Terri cheerfully. "That goes in C&D – Construction and Demolition." And with that, she pointed to an ominously overflowing dumpster standing outside the warehouse, but still on the grounds of the dump, the letters "C&D" spray-painted in orange on the side.

I walked outside to the C&D dumpster, which was sitting near a second warehouse filled with colorful bales of compressed and compacted trash. The industrial C&D dumpster was so tall that a small set of wooden steps had been erected to help those looking to dispose of their items. I mounted the steps, holding the chair in my arms, and then, looking around for direction and receiving none, I hurled the chair up and over the edge of the dumpster and onto the mammoth pile of trash.

I stood there for a moment, looking up at what I'd done and at what others had thrown in before me: charcoal grills, punctured inflatable rafts, insulation, more plastic lawn furniture. And then I turned around, descended the steps, and got back in my uncle's truck.

❧ ❧

Although most people understand the impulse for our year of no buying, when hearing about our adventure, they often ask us why. They are looking for the origin story. I believe that moment on the steps may be it. It was, I think, my own personal trash moment. After launching that chair into its long future among our planet's trash, I could see only two options. The first was despair; my default response in situations like this. I can't un-see the C&D dumpster, but I can't un-own all that I have. I can only chase the problem around and around in my head. The second option is denial, which I like to alternate with despair – just to mix it up. It is quite possible that we came home from the dump that day, piled in a boat, and pulled our kids and their friends around the lake in an inner tube that will one day, undoubtedly, end up in the C&D dumpster.

Despair and denial are downstream responses. They are just me, splashing around waist-deep in the mess I've made. Perched on those precarious little stairs, standing in the middle of the giant mess we had collectively made, I needed a third way – an upstream approach. This, of course, turned into our year of no buying. Our logic? We can't get out of the mess we're in, but we can stop making it worse. It was a first step.

The next step is messier and more difficult. To meaningfully process the waste I produce, I cannot continue to be a tourist, existing at a comfortable remove. Effective waste management requires intimacy with garbage; there is no 'away.' Like the Trash Pirates, I am going to have to dive in and get elbow deep. This closeness means fully rinsing the jar of marinara before tossing it in the recycling, scrubbing away the tomato sauce crusted into the ridges at the mouth of the jar. It means combing the sand at Beach Clean-Up Day, pincher tool in hand, squinting at a small piece of rubber and willing it to be a deflated balloon. It means mixing cat litter into cans of leftover latex paint, and leaving them to dry before scraping them out. It is tedium, and mess, and time I do not have. But I'd better find it. Because right now Terri, the Trash Pirates, the Zabbaleen – they are keeping the trash moving and the planet alive. Theirs is salvific work, their hands so much cleaner than my own.

CONSIDER THE LOBSTER

"A home is like a reservoir equipped with a check valve: the valve permits influx but prevents outflow," writes E.B. White in his 1957 essay, *Good-bye to Forty-eighth Street*. "Under ordinary circumstances, the only stuff that leaves a home is paper trash and garbage; everything else stays on and digs in." The essay chronicles the days leading up to his move out of a New York apartment, and opens with a reflection on how it is that he and his wife have come to own so much. "I have no sharp taste for acquiring things," White observes, "but it is not necessary to desire things in order to acquire them. Goods and chattel seek a man out; they find him even though his guard is up." White goes on to list the items that have "sought him out," including ballpoint pens, memo books from the bank, a log bearing the marks of beaver teeth (the gift of a reader), and a ceremonial hood bestowed upon him for an honorary degree. With his signature sense of humor, White concludes, "What I really needed at the moment was the beaver himself, to eat the hood... I shall never wear it again, but I have too weak a character to throw it away."

Coming across this essay was, for me, both relieving and troubling. Having asked myself more than once how we had managed to accumulate so many things, I was hungry for answers. I wanted to understand how we got into this mess.

According to White's analysis, acquisition represents only part of the problem. In addition to the many items we had purchased, goods and chattel had sought us out, and we hadn't fought one bit. Plastic army men had infiltrated by means of birthday party goody bags. Antique glass punch bowls were passed down as mothers and mothers-in-law downsized. Neighbors dropped by with mud-caked soccer cleats outgrown by children of their own. White's read on our situation served as absolution. Our sin was not so much active consumption as passive receiving. The news came as some relief.

At the same time, it was impossible to ignore the fact that it takes two to accumulate. Sure, people might pass along their goods, but we were taking them in with open arms, and – even worse – forming attachments, ultimately leaving us unable to part with them. These attachments, White seems to suggest, expose a human (and perhaps especially writerly) penchant for sentimentality. "As I sit here this afternoon in this disheveled room, surrounded by the boxes and bales that hold my undisposable treasure," White tells the reader toward the end of the essay, "I feel an onset of melancholy."

∾

I know this melancholy firsthand. Over a decade ago, I helped my mother move out of my childhood home. The job was large, but my mother – a paragon of organization and decisiveness – was up to the task. Like a general, she marched us from room to room, isolating first the specific territory in need of conquering, and then breaking down the tasks required to do so. We worked with precision as our Discard, Keep, and Donate piles grew steadily higher. Crawl space, linen closet, den bookshelves were empty in short order. We were in a groove. Sentimentality didn't stand a chance.

On the fourth day of cleaning, we moved operations to the

dining room. Trash bag and broom in hand, my mother walked straight over to the sideboard and yanked on a cabinet door. It sprang open with a pop to reveal a space crammed so full of cocktail napkins, that they exploded forth and fluttered like confetti to the floor upon release. A pale lilac from my sister's high school graduation party, a bright kelly green from what must have been a St. Patrick's Day affair, stately gold from my grandparent's fiftieth anniversary, an autumnal floral pattern from what was likely the Thanksgiving brunch we gave the year my father died. Momentarily stunned by the new and haphazard mess, my mother froze. And then, for the first time in four days, she stopped. She put down the broom and made her way to the floor, landing in the midst of the colorful mess. Sitting there on the ground, she began slightly rock back and forth, silently laughing a laughter that eventually built into sound, and then, as is her way, into tears. "Well, here it is," my mom gasped after a few moments, seated on the floor laughing and crying as she sifted her hands through the fallen napkins, "our history." Grabbing for a poinsettia Christmas napkin, she reached behind her glasses to dab at the corners of her eyes.

The moment took both of us by surprise. Prior to the napkin explosion, we had been engaged in an efficient campaign to purge and sweep clean. Ever the loyal soldier, I followed orders, working fully with my head, believing it was my job to decide the fate of individual items. Only one of these green striped mittens? Throw it out, no one needs only one mitten. But in clearing out the clutter, we had also demolished a thousand little archives cataloged in the corners of my childhood home. Every singleton mitten in the bottom of the closet was a clue, the first word of a story we still owned. The layers of cocktail napkins in the dining room spoke about time like layers of earth. Without these prompts and artifacts, how would we ever remember?

It is a popular minimalist maxim to suggest we carry only what we need. Which is to say that if I have forgotten what happened to that other mitten, if I haven't thought about it in 15 years, there is probably a reason. I believe this logic holds for individual items. I wasn't really sad about the mitten. Instead, my sadness – my melancholy – lay in losing all that accumulation. I was closing the door on the grand library of my past, no longer able to browse among a host of hints and reminders. Any memories I took with me would now be removed from their context, sanitized and categorized in photo albums or labeled storage bins. In the final walk-through of the empty rooms at the end of the week, I was aware of the vague sadness that accompanies an extinction or the destruction of a spiderweb. The sense that something unique was gone and would not be back in the same way ever again.

Our houses hold our stuff. Our stuff holds memory and meaning. When the time comes to go, to rid ourselves of our homes and all they contain, we lose these chapters and their attendant footnotes. "In every place he abandons," White writes of a man moving on from his home, "he leaves something vital, it seems to me, and starts his new life somewhat less encrusted, like a lobster that has shed its skin and is, for a time, soft and vulnerable."

☙ ❧

If memory is the sacrifice of shedding our things, momentum is the gain. Somewhat less encrusted, it would seem, we are free to move. In the late 1990s, newly engaged and fearful of little, I made the dubious decision to quit a promising job in Chicago, and join John in the small college town where he had just started a graduate program. Having moved down a few weeks ahead of me, John had set up shop in our graduate housing. Thus, when the time came for me to join him, the only items left for me to bring – some clothes and a few remaining books – fit comfortably in the trunk of my ancient Toyota Camry. My actual departure was on a warm September day. Exhausted from late night goodbye-ing, I threw on a pair of sunglasses and sped off toward southern Indiana. The car flew down the highway.

I distinctly remember feeling light.

My ability to detach – from both my life and my things – had been inspired, in part, by another road trip I had taken almost a year earlier to visit a friend doing a year of volunteer service. At the time when many of my college friends had landed entry-level corporate jobs up and down the Eastern Seaboard, Dawn made the radical choice to move to the heart of the Appalachian mountains, and take up residence in a communal volunteer house. Along with the other volunteers, she was living a life of simplicity and service, delivering education, food, housing, and other basic services to those deeply in need.

One weekend, eager to escape my own urban job and life, I jumped in the car and headed south to visit her. The memories of the weekend remain vivid, among them, a late night trip to a holler deep in the woods, complete with fiddles, clog dancing and – I kid you not – moonshine. But perhaps the most vivid impression made on me was the life led by Dawn's fellow volunteer, Judy.

Judy was an older woman, approximately my mother's age. At this advanced point in her life she had chosen to forsake the comforts and trappings typical of many women her age – well-appointed homes with proximity to grandchildren, jewelry, art – for a small, single room in a house in the middle of a rural mountain community crippled by devastating poverty. There, she spent her days alongside the mostly younger volunteer corps, serving as both den mother and tireless advocate for those around her.

At first, Judy's life made 22-year-old me sad. Having never been exposed to these lifestyle choices, I could only see what I thought was missing. I was on a path of accumulation – apartment, car, job – and Judy's choices seemed precarious and lonely. Family and comfort, as I had been trained to recognize them, were nowhere to be seen. Judy's choices also put her on the path of the daily and real human suffering that comes from addiction, hunger, and despair. It was one thing for Dawn to try this for a year; Judy had been at the volunteer house for two years and wasn't leaving anytime soon.

As I observed her life over the course of the weekend, however, an alternative narrative began to develop. Judy woke up to each day with time to make a meaningful difference in people's lives and went to bed each night after sharing a meal with friends. Perhaps, most notably, almost none of the intervening hours entailed caring for her things. Unencumbered, she found the space and time to care deeply about others. Not just family and friends, but complete strangers in need of help. I thought about all these things as I drove north at the end of the weekend, and by the time the Chicago skyline came into view, Judy and her choices had migrated from unfathomable to something just shy of desirable. While I cannot draw a direct line between Judy and my decision to quit my job, discard many of my things, and move south with John the following year, I am certain she was somewhere in the mix.

❧

Lobsters molt more frequently when they are young, shedding their shells five to six times per year. As they grow older, they molt only once or twice in a year, as their hard shells becomes tight and restrictive. So it is with us, I think. Despite my admiration of Judy, aside from that first move south, I have not emulated her. Shedding my material goods in exchange for a life of freedom or service has increasingly proven to be too much to ask. With each child, each subsequent house, it becomes harder and harder to conceive of leaving it all behind and starting somewhere fresh and new. I have wondered, more than once, if encased in the shells of our things as we age, we lose not only momentum, but the vulnerability that allows us to identify with the pain of others. I worry that our things make us numb.

The lobster in the last line of White's essay puts me in mind of another famous piece about lobsters, in which David Foster Wallace explores the morality of killing and eating animals capable of feeling pain. Assigned to cover the Maine Lobster Fest for *Gourmet Magazine*, Wallace takes the opportunity to describe how lobsters, by virtue of clinging to the lid of their container and scurrying away from capture, appear to express a preference for not being killed. In addition to this pathos argument, he also relies on logos, noting that lobsters are covered with tiny hairs that increase their tactile sensitivity. Putting these observations together, he arrives finally at an ethos question: is it okay to kill and eat a lobster, or, for that matter, any sentient being?

While Wallace's presenting question remains urgent, I'm more interested in the fact that lobsters, despite their hard shells, are still quite capable of experiencing pain. This strikes me as intuitively true. The material goods that encase me have not made me immune to suffering in my own life or the lives of those around me. Rather than serve as a buffer, my things create a sense of continuity in which I feel connected to others, especially to those I never knew – those who came before or will come after. I am my mother's daughter – keeper of our family history and, thereby, our heirlooms – such as they are, and I'm also a writer. Like White, sentimentality holds sway with me, forms the root of my empathy. Over time, many of my items come to have a totemic value, reminding me not only of where I came from and who I am, but also what I am called to be.

If having things does not keep me from identifying with others, it does, I would argue, limit my sense of the ways in which I can act in response to their needs. In my very sedentary reality, I respond to suffering through certain established channels – monetary donations, clothing drives, shifts at a local soup kitchen – but I am not often in Judy's position, capable of taking a wailing child from the arms of an exhausted mother and quietly walking the room until they both calm down. A life grounded by material possessions keeps me from being overly proximate to pain, or nimble in my response to crises large or small.

If I believe this to be true, why is it that I am more likely to add to my larder than to pare down? Why not rid ourselves of all but our most meaningful things, and move our family into a smaller space, leaving more time and energy to tend to the world? I suppose it is because I remain unclear on this central question: are my goods grounding and humanizing me, ultimately connecting me to others, or are they layers of insulation protecting me from a difficult and traumatic world? Put differently, am I defined or confined by that which I own? On the advice of Wallace, I'll leave it there. "These questions lead straightaway into such deep and treacherous waters that it's best to stop the public discussion right here," he cautions at the end of his essay. "There are limits to what even interested persons can ask of each other."

FOOTPRINT

I t is three minutes before we need to leave for summer
camp when Elliot, my eleven-year-old nonchalantly says,
"My shoe is annoying me." A quick check of said shoe
reveals a large hole in the sole. Yes, a hole.

"Elliot!" I exclaim, staring at the sole of his gray Nike sneaker in disbelief, "How long has it been like this?"

"Oh," he says, thinking a minute, "well, I guess, like, most of
camp."

⋘⋙

As of July, a full six months into our no buying commitment,
our surface agreement had held. Despite their initial doubts, my
family played along. The rules of engagement were adhered to
and, miraculously, nothing new had been purchased. More importantly, as I saw it, the year had amounted to much more than
rule-following. Our decision meant time spent on creation and
community rather than consumption. We were cleaning and repurposing, and I finally had taken the time to discover what was
in the mystery boxes in our garage. Halfway through the year, I
felt ready to declare our experiment an unqualified success, in
both the letter and spirit of the law. We weren't just getting by,
we were getting better.

Shoes, though, presented a niggling problem. Growing boys

have growing feet, and older brothers rarely leave shoes in hand-me-down condition. I knew that the boys were going to need new shoes at some point in the year, but I wasn't ready to break our no buying streak. Until the morning Elliot presented his holey shoe, I had chosen to ignore the problem of growing feet.

৵৲৽

In 1996, two Canadian economists coined the term *ecological footprint* as a way of describing our ecological and environmental state of being. We hear this term and its cousin, "carbon footprint," so often that it is possible to forget that the concept is grounded in a real calculation. Our ecological footprint, simply put, is the math that tells us how quickly our collective demand for resources is outpacing the planet's ability to renew itself after meeting that demand.

The work of these economists has found expression at the Global Footprint Network, a California-based nonprofit providing data to world leaders to inform their climate-related deliberations. The Global Footprint Network has also popularized "Earth Overshoot Day," which is the specific date in the calendar year at which point we – the general mass of humanity – have "spent" our consumption budget, and the earth needs the remainder of the year to regroup and process all the waste we have already produced and regenerate the resources we have depleted.

As of the writing of this essay, the Global Footprint Network suggests our collective overshoot date is July 29th.

৵৲৽

It is past time for us to be in the minivan en route to summer camp, but I am still in the basement digging around for duct tape to patch Elliot's shoe. Not finding any, I grab a roll of electrical tape and run back upstairs. Elliot has his shoes on and is seated on the ground, misting his face with his PowerAde water bottle. "Here," I say, plopping down on the floor next to him, "give me your foot."

Elliot's summer camp is sports-themed, and as I sit and patch his shoe, I find myself wondering how the electrical tape will hold up under the pressures of the soccer, football, and wrestling rotations. More importantly, I wonder how my repair job will serve him during basketball, the primary joy of Elliot's life.

Sitting there crisscrossing too-thin strips of black electrical tape over the hole, I don't know whether to laugh or cry at the absurdity of the self-imposed deprivation. What the heck are we doing? What, exactly, are we trying to atone for? In the grand scheme of things, our no- buying efforts weren't going to add up to much.

❧

Ecological math will exhaust you. Over the last few years I have begun to weigh, on an hour-to-hour basis, the relative value of my convenience against the longer-term ramifications of my waste. It's a line of thinking that started innocently. I brought my thermal mug to our local café so as to not incur the cost of a disposable coffee cup. I told the person taking orders at our favorite Thai spot that I didn't need plastic utensils with my delivery. "It's okay," I replied to the cashier at a nearby boutique, "I don't need a bag, I'm parked right outside." All this felt right, like I was contributing to some larger good. The drinking fountain and water bottle filler at our local YMCA did some of my calculating for me. With every splash of water dispensed into my bottle, it provided a digital readout in the top right-hand corner of the machine, updating me on the good news: *This machine has helped to eliminate the waste from 15,867 disposable plastic containers.*

Despite its virtuous intentions, this line of thinking had slowly begun to manifest in a kind of existential anorexia; an overriding will to disappear, to slowly erase my presence on the planet. Now, instead of forgoing the coffee cup, I had begun to think about skipping my trip to the cafe in favor of brewing my own pot of coffee at home. But while saving gas and preventing the possible use of a disposable cup, this decision also consigned me to my own company, rendering me, essentially, invisible.

Zero-waste anything sounds so good, but left unchecked it can develop into a kind of functional nihilism. The more I tried to extract us from the negative implications of consuming, the more extreme my line of thinking became. I began to see myself in the character of Walter Berglund – the protagonist of Jonathan Franzen's enviro-centric novel *Freedom* – a man so enmeshed in ecological math that he is undone by the wasted water of an unnecessary toilet flush. Walter's cause? His raison d'etre? Zero-population growth; the effort to limit the number of live births to the number of deaths in a given year.

Here is the notion of the ecological footprint run amok; for Walter and the zero-population crowd, life has become incompatible with being alive.

≈≫

After another day at camp in the holey shoes, Elliot asks if we can order him a new pair. We get on Amazon for the first time in months, and after extended deliberation, Elliot selects some black and white basketball shoes. I am delighted to discover, as the electrical tape on the soles of the gray shoes hasn't held too well, that the new pair will be on our front step the following morning. I go to bed feeling relieved as the rest of the week has rain in the forecast. But I also feel silly and defeated, like the shoes are the beginning of the end. We are on our way to becoming consumers again. Surely, I think, a more resolute family would have solved this problem without their credit card.

The shoes arrive the next morning as promised, and Elliot is thrilled. He puts them on in our front hall and begins making fade-away jumpers with a ghost ball, pantomiming defense against an invisible opponent. He models them for his brothers, and for possibly the first time since the start of summer camp, remembers to change out of the t-shirt he slept in without having to be reminded to do so.

As predicted, it rains heavily that morning, requiring campers to navigate a soggy playground before making it inside the school gym where camp is being held. From the car I watch Elliot gingerly sidestep puddles to protect his new shoes. Ultimately, he gives up in order to keep up with his friends who are dashing through the rain toward shelter. Mud flies up over his shoes and splatters his socks as he darts across the field.

Later that afternoon I come down to find Elliot in the kitchen, one brand new, muddy shoe sitting sole-down on the counter, the other lying on its side in the sink. A brown footprint mars my pristine white countertops. Globs of mud dot the basin of sink. "Elliot!" I snap at him, "What are you doing? You don't put muddy shoes on the counter!"

Elliot looks up at me, startled, and then holds out a ragged, soaked paper towel saturated with green dishwashing liquid. The water from the faucet continues to run full bore into the sink as it slowly dawns on me: Elliot is attempting to clean his new shoes.

❧

The Global Footprint Network has on its website a calculator that allows you to determine the date of your personal Earth Overshoot Day. Factors that go into this individual calculation include the frequency of your travel by both car and plane, your home energy use, and the amount of processed food you eat. My own Overshoot Day is May 26. Apparently I burn through my yearly allotment of resources two months faster than the whole of humanity. To allow the earth time to make up for the speed of my consumption, I would need to spend just over seven months dark and grounded. And because I live in Chicago, cold.

After you get the results from the Personal Overshoot quiz, a quick follow-up survey pops onto the screen, asking how you feel about your date, and gives you a range of emotions to choose from. Like a student who, despite sincere efforts to pass, just failed a test, I clicked on the blushing emoji next to "Embarrassed." And here's what the ecological whiz kids at the Global Footprint Network had to say to me:

> If you're thinking, "My Footprint is so high,
> I'm a terrible person!" STOP THAT! RIGHT NOW!
> Unless you're living in the carbon fast lane, there's
> no reason to be ashamed. Being alive isn't a crime.

The bubble of text goes on to state that consumerism isn't the only problem; cities and governments need to make larger structural changes. By pointing the reader in this direction, the response attempts to alleviate the acute guilt that can lead to individual paralysis.

What the survey doesn't say, but clearly implies, is that consumption is synonymous with life.

◦≈◦❧◦

It's difficult to untangle the issue of how much we consume from when and why. I am starting to wonder if, by not buying, our family addressed these questions in the wrong order. Or, maybe we took them on in the only order we could. Perhaps it wasn't until we mastered basic subtraction that we could do advanced math.

If, in this moment of global crisis, there is a justifiable kind of consuming, Elliot's shoes might be it. To consume them was to meet a need, of sorts. But it was also to give him distinct pleasure, and to draw out from him thoughtful care in return. Elliot's impulse to clean his shoes may have been the result of not consuming just long enough to feel a real desire and to once again value things. It may also be that Elliot simply loves basketball, and to put clean white shoes on his feet was to magically power up his outside shot and increase his speed. The sparkling shoes, a secret source of power.

I am not sure how to factor these variables into the footprint equation, but they appear to matter a great deal. If consumption is an inevitability of existence, then it would seem we must develop the discipline of choosing wisely alongside the discipline of choosing less. We are never going to be able to completely zero it out. To erase my footprint, and the footprints of those around me, would be to erase, in some measure, the evidence of our existence, the joy of being alive. I am not quite ready to go that far.

BUYING BIG BIRD

On Halloween, my son and his seventh grade friends decided to go trick-or-treating as the Sesame Street gang. Grant, a small redhead, was an obvious Elmo. Kirby would be Cookie Monster (obvious, too, if you know Kirby), and Theo, a loveable Oscar the Grouch. Foster, the tallest of his friends, was assigned the role of Big Bird.

Securing a Big Bird costume presented a problem, but seemingly not an insurmountable one. Besides, who is going to tell a seventh grader still willing to dress in costume, and a Sesame Street costume at that, that he can't be Big Bird? I was determined to figure out a way to get Big Bird to happen without consuming.

My first idea (read: fantasy) was to make the costume myself. Here, I should make a disclaimer that craftiness, in general, is not in my wheelhouse. There's a reason my preferred artistic medium involves only a computer and my brain. But every so often, I engage in some serious self-delusion and decide that I have the capacity and/or desire to craft. Big Bird occasioned one such episode.

I made Pinterest my initial stop. Like many online phenomena, the real purpose of Pinterest still eludes me. But it's a highly visual medium and entering "Big Bird Costume" in the search window yielded a blur of bright yellow, accented by orange, pink, and blue. I was hopeful.

From the Pinterest "wall," I selected a YouTube video hosted by a cheerful young woman who, inspired by the availability of 99-cent yellow feather boas, had backed her way into a Big Bird Halloween costume. With ping pong balls; black, blue, and pink paint; a glue gun; and some yellow fabric, she created a sexy Big Bird approximation in which she wore a strapless yellow halter dress, accented by the boa and Big Bird fascinator complete with eyes and beak set at a jaunty angle on her head.

I stayed with her through the construction and painting of the ping pong eyes, watching even through the glue gun maneuver that resulted in the yellow felt beak. But I felt something inside me give up as she threaded elastic through yellow fabric to construct the top of her dress. I was in over my head, out of time, and not actually in need of a dress. I closed out of Pinterest.

Next I tried our middle school listserv. I don't really like posting to the listserv. Even Replying All to an email makes me a little uncomfortable. Maybe it's just the sense that I don't need to bother everyone with my stuff, or that I feel exposed – I don't know. But I don't like it. So you can imagine the discomfort I felt when hitting send on the following post:

Long shot...does anyone happen to have a spare Big Bird (as in Sesame Street) costume or mask lying around that they'd be willing to lend out this Halloween? Size adult-small or child-large. If so, feel free to reach out to me directly! Many thanks.

I got a lot of great responses like, "We don't but would like to see you on Halloween if you find one!" Alas, none of them yielded Big Bird.

In a last desperate effort, I decided to hit up Lost Eras, a creepy and fascinating antique-meets-thrift store located on the sprawling first floor of a flat iron building in the Chicago neighborhood of Rogers Park. At least three of Lost Era's many rooms are devoted entirely to costumes, and one gets the sense

that their use is not limited exclusively to Halloween. When
a mid-October work meeting brought me within blocks of the
store, I felt it was fate. I parked and ran in, ignoring the pay-
by-phone parking meters (no time!). I was certain that Big Bird
would await me, and that the costume fee, plus a dry cleaning
bill, would constitute the extent of our Halloween investment.
I'd be out the door in a jiffy.

The first room I entered was filled floor to ceiling with costumes: big, purple Barney heads; floppy, rubber Darth Sidious
masks; blue satin Uncle Sam jackets paired with the requisite
red-and-white striped pants; and a rogue coffin shoved between
the overstuffed racks. Again, I was hopeful. Surely Big Bird was
in there somewhere.

But three rooms, an Oscar, six Elmos, and several Pikachus
later, I came to the conclusion that there was no Big Bird to be
found. I was out of luck and maybe also a little relieved. Then,
on my way out, next to a large brass bowl filled inexplicably
with white plaster hands, I noticed a single yellow feather boa.
For a moment, my YouTube muse beckoned. Couldn't I, she
whispered, make Big Bird happen with this boa, some felt, and
a borrowed glue gun? Then, checking my phone and realizing I
was going to be late getting home and still had no dinner plan in
the works, I suddenly knew with certainty that I was never going
to make or find this costume. I was going to be buying Big Bird.

❧

There is a chicken-or-the-egg reality to our relentless pace and
our constant consuming; it's hard to tell which came first. I am
a working mom with limited time and a family with twenty-first
century needs and expectations. We are booked solid and always
on the move. The quickest solution, more often than not, is to
buy something to meet our immediate need. Yet, the maintenance or replacement of our stuff – the very things we buy to

save time – takes up a good portion of our lives.

While I no longer believe that making a purchase necessarily saves me time, neither do I have enough hours in the day
to make what I might have purchased. And nor, apparently, do
I have the fortitude to go entirely without. Especially when it
means that the Sesame Street gang would be light one Big Bird.

It's hard to slow down alone. I think what we might really need, is to help each other get there; to agree to some small
kinds of culture change. Maybe an end to birthday party favors?
Maybe more Naked Lady parties, like the one in my neighborhood that functions as a massive swap meet of used clothes? I'm
not sure. I just know we need each other because our current
pace, coupled with our current appetite, is not sustainable. I
also know that after almost a year of my family trying this solo,
it is going to take a lot of willpower. More, evidently, than I can
muster on my own.

≈∾

The Big Bird story has a post-script. The next morning, driving
in the dark to an early morning meeting on the Southside, I
heard a radio interview with Caroll Spinney, the puppeteer who
has manipulated and voiced Big Bird since his inception. After
55 years on Sesame Street, Spinney was retiring. Ever the writer
in search of meaning, I was sure the universe was trying to tell
me something. John, ever the pragmatist, knew exactly what the
message was. Big Bird costumes were going to sell out. And fast.

He was right! Two nights later, when I logged on to pull the
trigger on the reasonably-priced Big Bird pajama costume I had
found online, they were sold out. As was a second option, a Big
Bird hoodie – gone as well. Like a recently dead celebrity, Big
Bird had suddenly acquired a lot of cultural cache. There were no
costumes to be found.

And so, in what can only be understood as a cruel cosmic
joke, I was forced to order the costume from the foremost online

and catalog purveyor of little plastic items, manufactured almost exclusively in China. Most of what this particular company offers is party favors and decorations, all of it plastic, brightly colored, and exceedingly cheap, making it the go-to stop for every teacher, room parent, bride, and birthday party planner trying to stay within a budget. In many ways, our no buying commitment could be understood as my one-woman stand against this very company. And there I was, entering my expiration date and CVC code on their website and calling it done.

The costume arrived on October 26th. Foster went out with his friends and there were great colorful pictures and memories made. Another Halloween went in the books. We chalked one up to happy childhood and tried not to think too much about the earth. But wouldn't it be nice if someday this were not a zero-sum game?

PAYING ATTENTION

Our downstairs bathroom contains a carabiner clipped around a supply of thin black ponytail holders. When I first opened the package of elastics, they exploded across the room, scattering hundreds of small black circles over the countertop and floor. My husband, who was standing behind me when the explosion occurred, handed me the carabineer that he happened to be holding, and suggested I hook the wayward products onto it. I followed his advice, gathered up the ponytail holders, and stuffed them onto the little clip. There they have remained.

I work out at an early morning exercise class, and require a ponytail holder to keep my hair off of my face. Before sneaking out of the house at dawn, I squat down in front of the sink, grope around in the dark until I feel the carabiner, grab hold of a new elastic, and roll it over my wrist for safekeeping until I arrive at the gym. This system seemed to be working fine until one morning, while squatting in front of the bathroom vanity in the darkness of the early morning, I noticed my supply was starting to dwindle. Five or six elastics hung loosely from the carabiner. I froze for a moment as it occurred to me that while I was daily removing a new ponytail holder from under the sink, *I was never putting one back*. Perhaps more startling? I had no idea what had become of the other elastics.

When I got back from the gym I began the hunt for the lost ponytail holders. I found a few in the shower where I'd removed them to wash my hair, and still more loose in the top drawer of my bathroom vanity. These hardly accounted for all that had gone missing, however, so I stopped to think hard about it. Before long an image began to take shape in my brain. It was an image of my tall 14-year-old son in his pajama pants, perched on the radiator next to my dresser. One of the endearing things about my eldest is that though he keeps his own counsel, he is, on occasion, given to moments of extended disclosure. Mostly late at night after his father and I are both in bed with our books, fighting to stay awake. Maybe he likes this time because he gets both of us at once, or maybe it's because it's late and a day of middle school is finally catching up with him. Maybe it's because his phone is plugged in downstairs, and it's time to look life in the face. But I digress.

The point is that Oliver comes in almost nightly and sits on our radiator to talk. And as the image of Oliver began to take shape in my mind, I could see something in his hands. Sure enough, he was holding one of my black ponytail holders. Fidgeting in his signature manner, he was twisting it around and around in his fingers while chatting with us, and eventually preparing to do the thing irresistible to boys everywhere. He was stretching it to fit over his left index finger, pulling it back with his right index finger, and firing.

I went upstairs to look under my bed. There they were; at least five ponytail holders that I must have taken off and left on top of my dresser, five ponytail holders that Oliver had absent-mindedly picked up and shot into the air during our nightly chats. I checked across the bedroom for those that might have flown further and found more against the back wall. I collected and returned them to the carabineer in the downstairs bathroom.

The ponytail incident was instructive. Had I not noticed

the disappearing elastics and sought out the missing ones, they would have been literally swept under the rug. Eventually they would have been vacuumed up, or somehow otherwise disappeared into the ether of my home. But ponytail holders are not toothpaste. Which is to say that despite the similar price point (Valu-Pack of 3 Crest Complete Whitening Plus Scope: $7.49; Scunci Effortless Beauty Large No Damage Elastics – 90 pc: $8.16), one is designed to be fully consumed over time, the other is not. We buy toothpaste with the intention of using it all up. But when, and more importantly *why*, had I started to treat the ponytail holders this way? Was it that there were 90 of them in an affordable pack? Was it that they came from a similar source – my local drug store – and were therefore classified as "disposable" in my mind? Was I just lazy? The correct answer appears to be all of the above. A modern-day abundance of cheap and readily-available goods has allowed me to slowly, and almost imperceptibly, expand my notion of disposability.

It's an odd revelation in a culture that seems, ostensibly, to be moving in the other direction. Consider the school lunch. When I was a child, I brought my lunch to school in a brown paper bag, its contents carefully packed by my mother. Each day's sandwich came in its own plastic bag, next to my carrots or apple slices in their own plastic bag, and my chips which came in their store-made plastic packaging. These three plastic bags sat atop the disposable juice box with attached plastic straw that served as the rectangular foundation at the bottom of the bag. My husband has similar memories, though his slightly more eco-conscious mother opted for wax paper wrapping. The idea, in either case, was that as the bell rang at the end of the lunch period, we could grab the entire mess, ball it up, and toss it in the trash on the way to class.

Today's lunch practices have changed. Most children in our town, including my own, go to school with an insulated lunch box filled with reusable plastic containers nestled alongside a thermos. Each morning I place sandwiches, chips, and fruit or veggies in their specific compartments while my children fill their water bottles. Lest you think all is green and happy where we stay, this change also means that the whole "ball it up and throw it out" part of lunch is over, too. We parents get returned to us half-eaten crusts of sandwich, entirely intact and un-touched pieces of fruit, or, at worst, unrecognizable wads of food we didn't pack to begin with. When tempted to get grumpy about any of this, I remember the plastic straw habit of my childhood and keep my mouth shut.

While certain disposable items are now frowned upon by the culture at large, I fear that many others, like my ponytail hold-ers, have quietly snuck in to take their place. Take, for example, our socks. I am in the habit of buying 10-count packages of white Hanes socks for my boys. Not only are they cheaper when sold en masse, but the whole process of post-laundry matching be-comes a breeze. Each sock has at least 19 potential mates. And as soon as one of the socks gets a hole, into the garbage it goes. We may spend a few weeks with an odd number of socks, but it all, as they say, comes out in the wash.

Socks were not always thus. In my mother-in-law's sewing basket, buried beneath fabric remnants and tangles of leftover thread, lies her grandmother's darning egg. Darning, a verb on the brink of extinction, is the act of mending a hole in fabric by weaving yarn across the hole with a needle. The darning egg is a wooden orb mounted on a small wooden handle, over which the damaged object, most often socks, would have been stretched to enable the seamstress to more easily make the repair. My husband's great-grandmother used her darning egg to mend her family's woolen socks to see them through the cold Minnesota winters.

I am not eager to return to this time. There is a long list of things I'd rather be doing than mending socks. But I sense I've somehow gone too far in the other direction. When, after a few months, our sock supply begins to dwindle, I run out to grab a new pack. And because they are hanging there, in an aisle adjacent to cosmetics and groceries, and because the price is right, socks have quietly slid into the category of disposable goods, right alongside my ponytail holders. Quickly used, quickly damaged, quickly replaced.

How to resist this slide in a culture that is constantly turning our attention in the other direction; encouraging disposability by offering us cheap updated versions of almost everything we own? Our sense of something as temporary and replaceable is so easily accelerated by the forces of marketing. How to take back the question of disposability for ourselves? The answer starts with paying attention.

In her 2019 treatise on attention, *How to Do Nothing: Resisting the Attention Economy*, author Jenny Odell describes what's at stake in our dwindling ability to focus deeply and notice what's around us. Not only are we more likely to be manipulated by social media and the marketing contained therein, but we also risk losing a sense of temporal and spatial context – our basic sense of place. As a result, she worries we compromise our ability to both think critically, and to understand the larger ecology of which we are a part.

Luckily, Odell believes attention is an act of will. Through conscious decisions to listen deeply, look closely, and think differently, we can, she asserts, begin to recover some of what we have lost. "What we pay attention to and what we do not," she writes, "renders our reality in a very serious sense." Odell, I believe, is right. Before I went looking for the ponytail holders, or stopped to notice my socks, their disappearance was not a symptom of disposability, but simply another mystery of modern life that I had no time to answer. Once I began to pay attention, my role in both their disappearance, and in relation to a larger cycle of consumption and waste was made plain. Where I had once seen singleton socks, I now saw an ecology of "things."

The answer to my disposability question was hiding in my minutiae, as is the answer to the question of how to respond. As I start to listen closely, there are phrases that tip me off to this more insidious kind of disposability, chief among them: "Just get online and order another." It may help to focus in on certain, boring, everyday items that we become determined to steward in a different way. So it was, in the end, with the ponytail holders. After collecting all those I could find around the house, including a fat, silver, sparkly one that I'm pretty sure wasn't mine to begin with, I clipped them back on the carabineer, and there they have remained. When one becomes stretched out and ineffectual, only then do I toss it in the trash.

A FEW OF MY FAVORITE THINGS

A pair of wooden arms sits atop the mantel in my living room. My grandfather, a Presbyterian minister, once gave a benediction in which he raised a fist and proclaimed, "This is greed," and then, turned an opened hand toward the sky, and added, "This, my friends, is love." The benediction inspired Fred Rose, an amateur woodworker in his congregation to return to his shop and begin work on the pair of sculptures that now reside on my mantle. Together they represent a sort of cubist rendition of the benediction; one, a clenched fist and its forearm emerging from a solid block of wood. The other, an open-handed partner that appears even more primitive with the same forearm, fingers, and thumb extending upward from the palm in five small smooth columns – no lines for knuckles or fingernails. There is no color aside from the wood, which is stained a warm, rich brown. I, who know nothing about these things, would say that it is walnut. I love them.

The minimalist lifestyle promotes the notion that stuff, writ large, is bad. It does seem, however, inexplicably human to attach to material things. The items that become most dear to us often have, in addition to aesthetic value, an almost indescribable sense of belonging. They either faithfully serve a purpose or, like my quirky hand sculptures, have found their right spot in a home. When your eyes come to rest on the object, a little feeling of smug certainty, so faint you barely register it, washes over you. Yes, you think to yourself, that is meant to be. It is this sensation, I believe, that the ubiquitous Marie Kondo is after when she directs her followers to ask of their items, "Does this bring me joy?"

The idea that a material object can bring us joy implies that, in some way, we are in a relationship with it. September 1985 marks the beginning of one such relationship for me. On the momentous occasion of my 12th birthday, I received from my parents a small Sony alarm clock called the Dream Machine. In terms of design, the Dream Machine was a device ahead of its time. A small white cube with domed round volume and tuning dials and a square face, the clock presaged all manner of Apple products.

The Dream Machine represented two kinds of independence. First, a parent need no longer wake me up in the morning. I was a grown woman of 12 and would be greeting the day on my own terms, woken by my alarm. Second, and far more important, in the 1980s, when music still had to be purchased in the form of albums or cassettes, the radio was an essential source of free, unlimited music. No longer held hostage to my father's taste in jazz, I could head up to my room, spin my little Dream Machine dial, and hear the Top 40 on B96 whenever I pleased.

The Dream Machine remained steadfastly loyal, sitting bedside and waking me up regularly throughout high school which, if you have or were a teenager, you will recognize for the impressive feat that it is. Naturally, when I went to college, the Dream Machine went too. Upon arriving at my freshman dorm, my roommate and I discovered campus housing installing a new door, as the football team had apparently taken down the original during training camp. When we returned to the room after the evening's orientation activities, we discovered that our door had been not only hung, but also hastily stained and finished, as had roughly everything else in its vicinity, including the Dream Machine, which henceforth had a yellowish cast and small brown flecks of stain along its top.

The speckled Dream Machine returned with me from college, and has woken me regularly every morning since. It has been the means by which I have gotten up for three a.m. feedings, dropped kids at ungodly hours to meet buses for tournaments and trips, made it to the airport for early morning flights, and arrived at work on time. Setting the alarm is now an act of muscle memory; it has been years since I have mistaken a.m. for p.m., or made the kind of error that results in morning chaos or missed appointments.

These days, with preselected music programmed on speakers throughout our house, the Dream Machine's radio function gets less play. The dial has migrated from Top 40 to our local public radio station and there it has stayed. In its old age, the clock has gotten cranky and occasionally decides, in addition to broadcasting public radio, to wake us with violent beeps of its alarm at top volume. The first time this happened, and we had both been jolted awake in shock and confusion, my husband rolled over and gently inquired as to why the Dream Machine was "shooting ear bullets" at him. We're still not actually sure why it does that, but usually some fiddling with the volume knob resolves the situation.

My clock now celebrates birthdays along with me. This fall, when I turn 46, the Dream Machine will turn 34, a remarkable age for a piece of 1980s technology, I think. Or perhaps not. Maybe this is exactly our problem, that these items have an incredibly long shelf life. They don't die. Rather, we just grow tired of them and dump them in ever-larger piles of junk. And here we arrive at the real mystery of the Dream Machine: why have I never grown tired of it? Why have I not replaced it with the alarm on my phone?

A social scientist friend once told me about the paradox of the cat's purr. To understand what it is that makes a cat purr, to really investigate, biologically speaking, scientists have to kill the cat. At which point, the cat no longer purrs. I am afraid this is the case with my Dream Machine. If I were to rationally dissect all the reasons that I cling to this outdated technology, the clock would surely lose out in favor of a multi-tasking device that is one-eighth the size, and automatically adjusts for Daylight Savings Time (the Dream Machine and I still spring forward and fall back manually). The mystique of the familiar would wither in the face of the practical, and I would have to say goodbye to my clock. I'm not sure this would serve me well.

Attachments to our things are important in that they culti-vate a very human potential for connectedness and depth that can be hard to come by at the speed we currently move. In his book, *Alienation and Acceleration*, German philosopher Hart-mut Rosa argues that due to the frenetic pace of modern life, we have become increasingly alienated from one another, from our things, and ultimately from ourselves. The second part of this argument, that we no longer feel connected to our things, sounds initially as though it should be a boon for minimalists. Rosa, however, argues the opposite, noting, "If you keep your socks, your car or your portable radio for decades, or at least for years... there is a great chance for them to become a part of yourself, and vice versa, of yourself becoming a part of them. A car you repaired ten times or even more is internalized by you. They be-come part of your everyday lived experience, your identity, and your history."

Due to the speed of technological change, and the relatively high cost of repairing versus replacing, Rosa observes that we are now less likely to care for, or even understand, the items we own. "I myself actually named the first PC I got," he reports. "I was sure that I would keep it for a long time, and I tried to make friends with it. ...Nowadays, I do not even know what type of computer I use... I don't care about how long I'll keep it. The same goes for my cell phone." This modern-day detachment from our things doesn't mean less stuff. It means we care less about these items, cycling through them at greater rates than ever before. In so doing, we further our sense of isolation and alienation.

Conversely, as I bestow human traits on my little clock, Rosa suggests, so shall this process humanize and ground me. There are few things in my house that bring me as much joy as my Dream Machine. It is technology I understand, a beloved item to which I have attached specific memories. The setting and sounding of its alarm bookend my days. Ironically, the only way to get more things like this is to *stop* acquiring, to allow our items to go the distance with us, and to resist the temptation of the new and shiny, choosing again and again in favor of the old and imperfect. Perhaps my grandfather was wrong in his benediction. To hold tight to something is not necessarily greed, but in the right circumstances, a kind of fidelity.

THRIFTY PIG

My generation, Gen X, had Depression-era grandparents, and the effect of their collective experience reverberated down through the years into our lives. Our elders saved scraps of tinfoil, discarded lipstick tubes, bits of twine, and decades' worth of *New Yorker* magazines. Back when long distance calling rates were a thing, my grandmother started her mental meter running at the beginning of every conversation. She would talk for no more than 90 seconds before starting her sign off: "Okay, Lovey, I'll let you go..." – cutting me off mid-sentence if need be. Haunted by memories of real scarcity, and the failure of large financial institutions, they stored up and saved up, keeping their assets as liquid as possible. My friend Joe's father recalls telling his parents that he was going to purchase a used car to drive cross-country in the 1960s. Joe's grandfather, concerned for his son's safety, offered to lend him the $2,700 that he needed for a new car. "C'mon Pops," Joe's dad said, "you don't have that kind of cash." To which his father replied, "Yes, I do. Just let me get my shovel."

These Depression babies had firsthand knowledge of a time when resources were in short supply. The squirrelish satisfaction with which they laid things aside wasn't your basic, modern day hoarding; it was grounded in the notion that less money spent means more saved, and was governed by the principle that waste is wrong. Full stop. Our own parents, born during or just after World War II, felt the effects of this dictum throughout their childhood. The "starving Armenians" cast a long shadow over their dinner tables, prompting them to clean their plates and not waste food. I have heard my uncle reflect on this phenomenon, wondering aloud these many years later, if he thought my grandmother was actually going to pack up his uneaten meatloaf and ship it abroad. Obviously not. Armenian children were a proxy. A way to indicate that waste had real, moral consequences.

Depression-era frugality can seem eccentric in the context of a modern life in which we place a much lower premium on curtailing our waste. To name a person as frugal or thrifty now, in these times of easy abundance, seems the verbal equivalent of a sly wink. It suggests a bent toward saving that borders on the excessive. Conversations with friends and family reveal that both words – thrifty and frugal – can be seen as a backhanded compliment, connoting someone who is clever but, perhaps more fundamentally, cheap. Their slippery feel was best captured by my mother-in-law who, when asked how she felt about the words, replied, "It would depend on who was calling me that."

Thrift and frugality were not always so tricky. The word thrift originates from the Middle English "thriven," or to thrive, and appears to also have been influenced by the Old Norse "prift," meaning prosperity. At some point in the 1500s, the prosperity of those with thrift became associated with an ability to save or economize, thereby moving us closer toward our current understanding of the word. Frugal comes from the Middle French "frugalis," which can be traced back to the Latin root "frux," for fruit. Some scholars believe that the Latin root itself was derived from a different Proto-Indo-European root, meaning to enjoy. Implied in both terms was the idea that to save was ultimately to succeed, to behave wisely and be financially rewarded. The thrifty and frugal would thrive and bear fruit. And heck, they might even enjoy it.

I think it's possible these words have only just recently acquired their more miserly overtone. In the 1970s, when it was still okay to leave your children unsupervised in the car for extended periods of time, my mother would crack the windows of our Chevy station wagon, remind us not to unlock the doors for anyone, and then run into our local pharmacy, Thrifty Drug. I feel as though this name would not survive a focus group today. Indeed, my childhood Thrifty is now a Rite Aid.

A sounder piece of etymological evidence can be found in the 1941 animated Disney short, *The Thrifty Pig*. A World War II, American propaganda film, this four-minute remake of the Three Little Pigs shows the pigs attempting to protect their houses from the Big Bad Wolf, who appears on the screen with a red Nazi armband and swastika-adorned hat. Practical Pig (the apparent hero of our film, despite the title) is shown in the opening scene with mortar and trowel, having been diligently working to build his house from bricks made of World War II savings bonds. As the wolf demolishes the straw and stick houses of the other pigs, they flee to the safety of Practical Pig's house. Try as Nazi Wolf might, he is unable to blow down the house made of savings bonds. In further defiance, the pigs then hurl the unused brick bonds at the wolf, sending him running away howling. The movie ends with the pigs dancing a jig around a piano in Practical Pig's cozy house, hardly the picture of the spare living we might now associate with thrift. Rather, thrift has saved the day and shored up the good life. The pigs are enjoying themselves and the community is better off.

This movement from thrifty as hardworking and heroic to thrifty as endearing and odd, suggests that the shift is not just in our use of the term, but in our overall relationship to the concept. The thrift of *Thrifty Pig* was to be aspired to, it was a virtue worthy of cultivation, one associated with a good life. The frugality of our grandparents, while at times manifesting in odd ways, represented to them a hard-won wisdom and forward-thinking attitude. A person with cash buried in their front yard is one step ahead of impending disaster. Reused tin foil means money to spend later on things that matter. Thrifty people are beating the system.

The frugal friends I have today tend to make only glancing, self-deprecating references to their behavior. Sure, people might brag about a Groupon deal, but hard-core thriftiness stays mostly under wraps. Perhaps the frugal among us sense that the rest of us are uneasy with outward, prideful displays of thrift. At some level, these people are spoiling our fun. A college roommate whose mother used to rinse and reuse Ziploc bags, once saw me doing the same at the sink in our apartment and told me it bothered her. When I asked her about it, she struggled to explain. The best she could offer was that the activity depressed her by bringing to mind a kind of dreariness associated with a childhood memory of her mother's chapped, red hands and the faint whiff of onions.

And here may be the place where thrift departs from the current minimalism that is all the rage. Simply put, it's not pretty. Every time I see a tiny house I am astounded by its small footprint, but I am also unfailingly impressed by its gorgeous décor. To join the minimalists is to cut back, but also, apparently, to exhibit great taste. To be frugal, on the other hand, is not just to cut back, but to use and reuse what we have. Wear and tear, and a whiff of onions is implied. All this makes thrift a much harder sell in an Instagram world.

❧❧❦

Among the items I failed to purchase before our arbitrary January 1st no buying deadline was some sort of rug for my youngest son's bedroom. Our house is old, and full of hardwood floors, and I was regretting that I hadn't managed to secure some kind of floor covering before we clamped down on purchasing.

A solution presented itself in the form of some friends moving into a new house. Their new home, a stately, renovated Victorian, was still empty at the time of our first visit and our voices echoed in the halls as we walked. Halfway through, I noticed that the echo was amplified by the fact that all the carpeting was ripped out, rolled up, and pushed against the walls. When I asked Richard about it he told me that the previous owners had pets, and that his own children were highly allergic. As a precaution, despite the relatively good condition of the old carpeting, our friends were replacing all of it.

I got into bed that night, said goodnight to my husband, and turned out the light. But just as I started to drift off to sleep, the spirit of my grandmothers Marcy and Ruth appeared before me in a vision. "Honey," Grandma Marcy said, in her thick Long Island accent, "go get that used cahpet." "Yes," Grandma Ruth concurred, "they'll bind it for you at the carpet store. It's very reasonable. Plus, Susannah," she added with her keen designer's eye, "it's Berber." And before I could ask them anything more, like how my grandfathers were, they were gone.

What to do when you have been visited by the Ghosts of Thriftiness Past? Obey, of course. The next morning I texted Richard: "So the carpet you're ripping out. Possible I could come get a scrap of it – roughly 4x8?" I felt awkward composing it and hovered a little over the little blue arrow icon before sending. All my hang-ups about thrift came rushing to the fore, and I felt a little silly in the asking, as though I were imposing my values on a friend. By scavenging among Richard's scraps, I worried that I was implying he was wasteful.

The problem was in my head. Richard invited me to scavenge with open arms. It took a little hunting, but Richard, his contractor, and I located a patch with no discernible odor or telling stains on the burlap backing. (A whiff of onion is one thing. A whiff of cat pee, another thing entirely.) The contractor sliced off

a section, rolled and tied it with twine, and Richard and I loaded
it in the back of my minivan. I drove directly to the nearby carpet
store, walked in and asked them how much it would be to bind
a piece of used Berber carpet. "Uh, we can do it," the carpet guy
told me, looking a little surprised, "but for just a little more you
could probably get a new area rug online. They're really cheap
and come in lots of colors and patterns. Try rugsusa-dot-com."

The forces of consumerism are multivalent. Not only had an
initial bout of self-consciousness almost derailed my thrift once
already that morning, but now the carpet guy had become yet
another barrier by encouraging me to buy new rather than reuse.
If I bought something new, he seemed to be hinting, it would
make both our lives so much easier. Worth noting? In directing
me to an unaffiliated website, *he wasn't even trying to make a
sale*. Instead, he was trying to help me in the way you might give
directions to someone who is lost. Just out of the goodness of
your heart. To him, I suppose, I must have appeared misguided
or benighted. "Here." I imagined him saying kindly, "let me show
you how the Internet works."

Fortunately, committed to our year of no buying, I was not
about to capitulate at Central Rug and Floors. "Thanks," I answered, "I'll just go ahead and bind the salvaged piece I have."
I retrieved the roll of carpet from my car, dropped it with the
salesman, and agreed to come back in two weeks.

When, two weeks later, we got the bound carpet back and
unrolled it across Elliot's floor, he was thrilled. and so was I.
The room remains, however, very un-Instagram-able, primarily
owing to the fact that I have also neglected to get any sort of top
cover or bedspread for his bed. For the time being, it's covered
with a lumpy bright white duvet that does not exactly work with
the off-white of the Berber that is now on his floor. None of
which really goes with the gray-green walls. The whole thing is a
bit ragtag and bland.

This blandness is not what I see when I walk into Elliot's

room. I see, instead, a covered floor. Some carpeting that's not in a landfill. A bit of money saved. My grandmothers' smiles. I see all this, and it gives me a sense of satisfaction. It's a certain kind of victory, and it makes me want to dance a little jig, Thrifty Pig style.

THE CUNNINGHAM GENE

My husband recently completed a DNA analysis, the kind that traces out his ancestry and explains his ability to tan but never burn. When the report came back, we discovered that not only is he pretty much exactly the mutt he thought he was (English/Irish, General European), but that he has more Neanderthal ancestry than most people. I am not sure what to make of this last bit of information.

Included in the report was a silly list of things that those in John's familial line are more likely to be able to do than the general population, including front and side splits. I am dubious, as I don't think I've ever seen John so much as touch his toes. The list includes other items that baffle me in that they are clearly genetic traits but the link is not obvious; they seem more a matter of taste or circumstance. His DNA relatives are 54% less likely to drink instant coffee than the general population, 23% more likely to own a dog, and 10% more likely to have lived near a farm when they were young.

In these days, when we are able to trace almost every single one of our proclivities, habits, vices, strengths, and skills back to our genetic make-up, I find it appealing to imagine that our relationship to our things could be explained as genetic predisposition. It is relieving to think there might be a "stuff" gene determining our appetite for acquisition; that my overfull basement is the result of inborn forces beyond my control. This nature versus nurture thinking lets me off the hook and somehow justifies our no buying decision. If we are suffering from congenital consumption-itis, a lifestyle change may be just what the doctor ordered.

When you want some science to support your wishful thinking, there is no better friend than Google. A search on genetic predisposition to owning turned up several studies conducted in the early 2000s that point to a genetic susceptibility to hoarding in patients with obsessive-compulsive disorder. These findings actually make sense to me. In our early (apparently Neanderthal) days, we were hunters and gatherers who progressed toward storage even as we were still nomadic. As long as 25,000 years ago, we began to weave plant fibers into baskets meant for carrying and stowage. It seems entirely possible that something in our genes could have gone a little wonky at this point, setting off a whole line of ancestors for whom a full basket would never be enough.

But what of the other segment of the population; the part for whom stuff holds exceptionally little meaning? They appear to be an understudied bunch. A Google search on "genetic predisposition to minimalism" yields no results. And yet, if there is something genetic that might pull us toward having, couldn't its opposite also be true?

When it comes to the desire to own, our family has one such outlier in Foster. Of my three children, Fos cares the least for material things – mugs with Nick Offerman's face notwithstanding. While my other two had attachment objects in their infant and toddler years, Fos had none – no shredded blankie or matted bear to be retrieved before bed. He had his thumb, which he sucked in a strange open-faced backwards manner (probably another genetic thing), and that was enough. Come Christmas, he would open a gift and proceed to play with the box in which the toy had come. As the middle child in our family, clothes flow through his drawers on their way from Oliver to Elliot, and he has yet to show much interest in what's there. He has not, so far, had the typical middle kid "I never get anything of my own" meltdown.

For a while now, I have been engaged in a study of Foster (n=1) in order to test my hypothesis that each of us could have a genetically-determined set point for acquisition; a biological explanation for our need to own. I have registered his expressed desire for things, rare though it is, and tried to observe what is driving it. I have also controlled for environment. Our boys have been raised in the same house, exposed to the same values and experiences, and received similar amounts and types of birthday gifts, allowances, and permissions in museum gift shops. Theoretically, they should all have their basic needs more than met and should therefore exhibit the same amount of "want," albeit for different things.

After a twelve year longitudinal study of my middle child, here is my central finding: the opposite of the desire to have is not the desire to have less. In other words, unlike my anti-stuff snit that launched us on the year of no buying, Foster doesn't have strong feelings about whether he owns too much or not enough. In fact, *he doesn't really care about the question of ownership at all.*

Foster does not want things. Preferring experience and appreciation to owning, he would rather eat chocolate and play board games. Or this: uncommonly talented at the arcade claw machine, he will maneuver the claw, painstakingly lift a ball or stuffed animal from the prize pile, remove it from the machine, and hand it over to his little brother who has been standing next to him staring fixedly the prize, practically drooling with anticipation. This scene appears, on the surface, like an exceptional act of brotherly love. Random parents loitering nearby have come up to compliment me about it. I can take no credit for

Foster's actions. For Fos, the experience is all.

My observations of Foster suggest that, at age 12, he has not completely renounced all worldly goods. The material object closest to his heart is his set of art markers purchased over many months from an art supply store near our house. Having at last acquired enough to complete a nuanced rainbow, he will spend time ordering and reordering them, arranging them on our dining room table in different arrays of color as he sets out to draw. On gray winter afternoons when he sits down with his markers and a stack of blank paper, his joy appears to come as much from the bright colors in front of him, and the potential for creation, as it does from the fact that the markers are his.

Given Foster's artistic nature, I have wondered whether this indifference to owning comes from what could be an inverse relationship between an ability to appreciate beauty and a desire to own. (If this were true, it would give lie to every antiquities-obsessed villain ever to darken the screen of an Indiana Jones movie; they all are transfixed by beauty and *still* want to get their hands on the goods. Nonetheless, let's continue with this theory of mine.)

More Googling suggests that art appreciation, difficult though it is to define, has a biological basis, and from there, it is a very short leap to genetics. A 2015 study published in the *Journal of Experimental Psychology* demonstrated an increased appreciation of complex works of art among study participants with a stronger visual working memory, a capacity that is a "heritable and relatively stable trait," according to the authors. For purposes of this essay (and my own peace of mind), I will cite this study as evidence that we may be genetically hardwired to perceive and enjoy the world in certain ways.

And now, a cobbling together of all my Googling: if it is possible that we could have inborn tendencies regarding both ownership (hoarding) and appreciation of beauty (aesthetics), doesn't it also seem possible that we could come into the world with one more dominant than the other? If I were a geneticist capable of mapping the genome, and I came across this trait, I would entitle it the Cunningham gene, in honor of the late *New York Times* fashion photographer Bill Cunningham, the archetype of the appreciator/non-owner category. Cunningham was a giant in the world of fashion, but the most unlikely kind. Famous for riding around on his bike, photographing high fashion and street fashion alike, Cunningham himself dressed in the same clothes each day, and lived in a sparsely-furnished studio apartment in Manhattan. Constantly fashion-adjacent, he had no need to own or dress in the clothes from the runway – only to be proximate to them, appreciate them, and capture them for others to see. A documentary about his life details an early period in which Cunningham dabbled in fashion design, creating fantastical hats shaped like sea creatures. That episode appears to be as close as Cunningham ever needed to come to a hands-on relationship to fashion. Like Fos, and others with the Cunningham gene™ (*TM* mine), creation and appreciation supplant the need to own. Based on our culture at large, I would say it is recessive.

Having concluded (manufactured?) this thoroughly unscientific review, I have to admit to feeling both self-justified in our no buying, but also a little guilty. I insisted my family join me on this journey with the belief that we were caught in something larger that we could not control, and that we needed to make a change. This still feels accurate. But Foster's indifference toward ownership was part of my calculus. I took his inability to come up with items for his Christmas list as evidence that our family had reached some kind of saturation point, that we were all "owner" types who had finally come to own too much and simply couldn't think of what to ask for next. Our baskets were more than full. In retrospect, I may have misinterpreted the data. Maybe Fos truly didn't crave anything at all. Maybe he was simply content.

As for the rest of us, the ones with the other, more dominant genes that drive us to have? We remain in need of something to rebalance us, to shift our attention away from ownership and toward experience and creation, to help us seek out the very contentment that seems to come so naturally to Foster. For the time being, I have prescribed a change in lifestyle; a halt to shopping and adding to the larder – a tactic designed to slow our impulse to grab hold. Something to help us stand at the claw machine and, for a minute, take our eyes off the prize long enough to watch, wide-eyed, as the action unfolds.

THE REBUILDING WAREHOUSE

Repair clinics have been popping up around my town. The basic idea is to bring the broken item lying around your house – the thing you are tempted to toss and replace – to the clinic to find a way to make it work for you again. Clinics have been held at both our local high school and at our local Rebuilding Warehouse, a nonprofit resale shop that exists to receive and repurpose the byproducts of home renovation – old cabinetry, tile, and fixtures. As home renovations are *de rigueur* on Chicago's North Shore, the Rebuilding Warehouse never has a shortage of inventory.

When I first heard about the repair clinics, the whole thing called to mind Luis' Fix-it Shop from Sesame Street. I foresaw genial men in leather aprons brandishing screwdrivers and bringing broken toasters, Lazarus-like, back to life. Neighborly kindness flowing out in every direction. I was reliant on this childhood image, as where I live, fix-it shops are a dying breed. The few left in my town tend to be specific to a single item and sport names that date from the phonebook era, like A-1 Vacuum Service Co. A few technology repair shops with names that reflect a more modern sensibility (ubreakifix.com) have sprung up, but if I wanted to repair my favorite coffee maker or ancient lawnmower, I'm not sure where I'd go.

The shift from repairing to replacing has occurred during

the span of my lifetime. As late as the 1980s, I was required to take a Consumer Economics course in order to graduate from high school. This class, tucked in the back of the vocational tech wing, in a classroom next to the auto shop, was taught by Mrs. Stern who hailed from somewhere in rural Indiana but, with her blonde bob, blouses, and skirts, seemed to have materialized out of one of the 1960s filmstrips she would often show in class. Mrs. Stern used the class to introduce us to the indispensable *Consumer Reports* and to instruct us on how to formulate a household budget. We learned how to balance our checkbooks using the ledger provided in the checkbook itself, and were educated in the important practice of filling out and mailing in the warranty card that accompanied most major purchases.

I spent most of those classes staring at the faded posters mounted on the cinderblock walls and watching the clock. In truth, I think I might have forgotten about the class were it not for a visit to my grandparents shortly after the semester ended, during which I happened to catch my grandfather heading out to the post office one morning. The rubber ring surrounding the base of his blender had broken and, having checked to make sure the blender was still under warranty, he was writing to the Oster blender company for a replacement ring. That moment was my Consumer Economics semester come to life.

I've since used the blender story to gauge, among my peers, how many of us today would still be likely to a) fill out a warranty card, even online, or b) email a company for a replacement part. A gets a resounding no. B runs the gamut; those with high-end blenders *might* make an effort to repair their item. For those with more workaday blenders, the broken blender goes into the trash, and its owner goes online to buy a replacement.

If fixing broken things rather than replacing them represents one kind of cultural shift, I now want to admit to another, more embarrassing one. There are items in our house that I would rather replace than *clean*. Take the clear plastic

shower curtain liners that surround the claw foot tub in my boys'
bathroom. (Please, take them...) After years of shower spray,
a greyish orange mildew has accumulated around the bottom
edges that no quick shot of cleaning product can now remove.
I have been told by well-meaning friends and relatives that a
mixture of vinegar and water in a spray bottle could solve my
problem. I would just need to a) take down the curtains, b) wait
for a nice day (I live in Chicago, remember), c) spread them out
on my back patio, d) attack them with the vinegar concoction
and a scrub brush, e) wait for them to dry, and then f) rehang
them. Or, I could simply run to Target and grab two new liners
and replace the old ones, thereby skipping steps B through E and
ending up with a nicer result.

The mildewed liners have stayed in place primarily because
I have boys who are not preoccupied with the aesthetics of their
shower experience. But the liners also remain because over time
they came to represent a paralyzing conundrum. Each time I
thought of cleaning the liners, I instead chose one of the 8,000
more pressing items on my to-do list. Each time I thought about
going to Target to get new liners, I conjured up the distinct
chemical smell of shrink-wrapped plastic folded in on itself, and
my heart sank. I wouldn't make the time to clean, yet I couldn't
pull the trigger to replace.

⁕

The choice to buy instead of fix or clean is borne of a culture of
affluence in which there is a dangerous combination of financial
abundance and limited time. Business becomes a justification
for purchasing everything from fast food to duplicate items that
we already own but run out of time to look for and locate in
our homes or rental storage units. It can explain at least part of
why the things in our closets, garages, and basements seem to
increase exponentially over time, yet it is only one of the many
ways that affluence lends itself to consumerism.

The 2008 financial crisis hit my mother-in-law's Florida community hard. In the inland development, filled with small pastel-colored ranch houses, many of her fellow residents found themselves upside down on their mortgages and needing to get out. By the time we made a spring break visit the following year, every third house had a For Sale sign in the front yard. And of those who managed to hang on to their homes, most felt an economic pinch as pension funds and retirement savings all but disappeared.

I remember feeling as though the sadness of the time was palpable in the thick Florida air. Mothers seemed to yell with more frequency at small children running up and down steep driveways. Older couples snapped at each other as they made their way through the heat and into their air-conditioned homes. Adding to the anxious and oppressive feel were rumors of a nasty pit bull in the neighborhood, able to break free from his leash. My mother-in-law had taken to carrying a small bottle of pepper spray with her in case she encountered the pit bull on her daily walk.

During this same spring break visit, I spotted her putting on her shoes one Friday evening, preparing for what I assumed was a rare second walk of the day. Maybe, I thought, she knows the pit bull has bedded down for the night. Instead I discovered that she was heading out for "Garage Sale Night." Intrigued, I accept-ed the invitation to accompany her. As we rounded the corner of her driveway and took off down the street, she explained that on Friday evenings, various people in the community opened their garage doors, set up a few tables, and placed their worldly goods out for sale. In making the rounds on past Fridays, she had scored an attractive butter dish and a stylish terra cotta planter, both at rock bottom prices.

That particular Friday evening nothing struck our fancy as we perused the few houses that had items out. But this rotating garage sale, functioning essentially like an ongoing neighbor-

hood swap meet of household goods, was my first real sign of
the shadow economy that had begun to operate in her neighborhood. In 2009, in this little Florida development, neighbors had
begun to rely on an informal barter system to cut costs in tight
times. My artistic mother-in-law gave drawing lessons to the
teenage boy who lived next door. In exchange for these lessons,
he mowed her lawn. A woman down the street was cutting hair
out of her home and accepting rides to the grocery store or doctor as payment. Divided hosta plants had real currency, as did
some delicious home brew.

Bartering is not so common in my community, although
it happens occasionally. I have a graphic artist friend who is
great at it – she recently traded a logo for some free sessions
with a personal trainer. But on the whole, I don't know that it's
a regular practice. Plain old borrowing is not so common either.
I receive the occasional text asking if anyone can lend a sport
coat or pair of boys' dress shoes for a one-off wedding or funeral,
but I would not say that the sharing of resources is a regular or
intentional thing.

"Neither a borrower nor a lender be," Polonius cautions his
son in *Hamlet*. But I have observed that most people in my community have no problem being the lender. People who exist in
my land of plenty are more than willing to share, if conditionally,
the goods that they have. The corollary? We loathe having to be
the borrower. No one wants to be the Homer Simpson to their
neighbor's Ned Flanders, always mooching and returning every
item in worse condition than when they received it. We insure
against this possibility by purchasing our own items – wheel-
barrows, power washers, handbags for dressy affairs – and then
lending them out as requested. So much better, we think, to be
the bountiful provider than to assume the role of the person in
need.

I live on a tiny street that runs the length of one block; there
are only five houses on our whole street. In Chicago, which has

an average annual snowfall of 36-inches, each of the five households on my street feels justified in owning its own individual
snow blower. The great comedy of this redundancy is revealed
when the first person out on a snowy day, in a show of neighbor-
liness and chivalry, clears the whole block of accumulated snow,
thereby obviating the need for others to come out with their own
machines. We are happy enough to share the work, but we are
reluctant to share the object itself. We each want our own snow
blower.

What is it that we are so afraid of? My guess is that each
of us would tell you we need our snow blower to clear our own
driveway, and that we wouldn't want to burden a neighbor with
that request. But this problem could be worked out. Gas could
be purchased in exchange for lending the machine. Teenage kids
could be offered as free labor. There could be ways to make the
borrowing more palatable. All of this, however, would put us in a
different kind of relationship to each other. We would need one
another.

At the root of an affluent reluctance to borrow is a fear of
dependency. The illusion of complete self-reliance is so comforting, and it comes at the relatively low cost of our own extension
ladder. Self-reliance is, of course, only an illusion; our lives and
choices are all connected. It takes only a small change in circumstance – a twisted ankle, a lost job, 2008 – to make our interdependency plain. Try as we might, we cannot buy our way out of
this condition.

∽≈∾

I took note of these lost arts, these alternatives to consuming, as
during our year of no buying I was having to relearn them; to remember anew how to ask to borrow something, or how to clean
and patch an object I would have otherwise replaced. My skills
were rusty and my efforts awkward. I needed, it seemed, lessons
in both basic carpentry and interpersonal

dependence. It was a tall order. The Rebuilding Warehouse sounded like a logical place to start. In the name of research, I decided to check it out. Lacking an item in need of immediate repair, I opted instead to attend a reuse workshop, designed to teach participants how to make a rug out of used t-shirts. I recruited a few friends to come along. It should be noted that the verb "crochet" appeared nowhere in the description.

Crocheting a circular rug out of old t-shirts is not the stuff of beginner crafting and, therefore, not the easiest thing to accomplish in a two-hour workshop. The process first involves a series of elaborate cuts to the t-shirts to create a seamless ball of "t-shirt yarn." A bit like making a paper snowflake, one disastrous misplaced snip can result in disconnected fragments. useless, in this case, for rug making. With no ability to visualize how my cuts were ultimately moving me toward a single strand of fabric, I was left to blindly follow an older woman at the adjacent table who kindly put down her own project to assist me in this first, fundamental step.

Then, there was the actual crocheting. Learning to hold a crochet hook so that you can move it fluidly in and out of the yarn takes practice, and it doesn't get any easier with the giant, plastic hook necessary for t-shirt rug making. Prior experience helps. My friend, Joanna, educated in the Waldorf tradition (emphasis on crafting over reading, she explained) was three rows into her rug, while the rest of us were still trying to figure out a basic stitch. "Maybe just skip the hook and try with your fingers?" she suggested to us as she plowed on, stopping occasionally to pull out our stitches and correct our mistakes. An hour into the class. and struggling to tug her hook through the center of the rug, my friend Tina looked directly at the instructor and declared, "This is not bringing me joy."

I came out of the workshop with the start of a rug – a colorful, frisbee-sized disc made from three old concert t-shirts that had once fit a younger, concert-going me. I brought it home and

showed it off to my husband and children who were watching
TV. They were genuinely impressed, which was most definitely a
statement on the infrequency of my crafting, and not the quality
of my mini-rug. I joined them and continued to work on the rug.
As I rhythmically pulled and looped, I allowed myself fantasies
of winter nights spent in front of the TV, my hands busy repurposing our worn and tattered clothes.

This, of course, will never come to pass. (First clue: I hardly
ever watch TV.) My project stalled. Eventually, several weeks
after the workshop ended, I clumsily knotted the loose end of
my disc and deemed it a trivet. I slid it underneath a plant in my
front hall, and there it has stayed.

In fact, as far as I can tell, there was only one person who
left the workshop having made any meaningful progress. It was
the older woman who had helped me make my cuts at the outset.
Unlike the rest of us, she seemed at home there, sitting comfortably at her place, glasses perched on the bridge of her nose and a
stack of navy t-shirts arranged in front of her. Once given license
to start by our instructor, she cut through them with startling
efficiency. Her hands were dark and a bit gnarled, but when she
began crocheting her rug, they moved with assurance as though
with a will of their own. In the casual conversation that built up
over the course of the workshop, we learned that she was a quil-
ter and also knew how to knit. Her rug took shape quickly, a rich,
deep blue that I imagined warming up a grandson's bedroom.

And still, while accomplishing all of that, she had been so
gracious to my group. She took time with us. After showing me
how to make cuts, she stopped several times to guide my friend,
Amanda, helping her with the tricky maneuver required to
round out the small circle at the center of the rug. She had laid
down her own work to assist Tina, who had unraveled portions
of her circle and was attempting to begin again. She quietly
supported the instructor with gentle suggestions, and all the
while kept patiently and persistently at her own rug. There was

a generosity to her kindness; never once did we sense that by helping us, she was losing something for herself. Instead, as we worked, her circle grew larger and larger.

OUTFITTING OLIVER

Today is Oliver's high school orientation. As it happens, Oliver will be attending my alma mater, a giant public high school that holds within its walls some of my all-time favorite memories. This afternoon is therefore inducing in me a familiar mixture of nostalgia and apprehension. There should be a word for that. It's a mood that characterizes a lot of my parenting.

For his part, Oliver is mostly calm in the face of this huge change. He will not drown in the enormity of his school, the country's single biggest high school campus under one roof. He is only a text away from locating everyone he knows. Gavin's locker is in X place, Harrison and Nick have lunch in Y cafeteria. He may not ever see them, but he'll know they are there. Oliver is also a non-anxious kid, not prone to overthinking moments like this. Thus, it has not been Oliver, but rather other parents I know, who have been curious about Oliver's high school launch. Of utmost concern, given our no buying commitment, will we be getting him new clothes for the start of school?

Some of this intense questioning has to do with Oliver's un-common height. He hit six-foot-two while still 13, and is working his way toward six-foot-three, though the vertical growth has slowed in recent months. In its place there has been some filling out. There is now a second hairy-legged, deep-voiced man under my roof. I have been known to startle at the sound of his voice.

Oliver's filling out means that wearing his father's clothes is an option for him, news that does not thrill John. Did I mention that Oliver is left-handed and prone to knocking things over? (Actually, it's not just Oliver; a friend with two daughters recently observed of a dinner with my boys, "There is a lot of spilling happening.") When John hands a piece of clothing over to Oliver, there is no guarantee how it will look upon return, but chances are high that you will be able to identify at least one of Oliver's last three meals. John, whose daily work uniform – a button-down shirt, sweater, and jeans or khakis – was already showing signs of wear from going without replacement, is appropriately wary of Oliver's gradual encroachment on his closet.

The question of whether Oliver's clothes will fit him is one reason people are curious about our plans. But there is another concern at work. Implicit in the question is the notion that one is *supposed* to mark the start of the school year with new clothes. And as I type the sentence I can feel, almost viscerally, how strongly I believe this myself. Back-to-school shopping was an annual childhood ritual for me. To be sure, it involved negotiating with a mother who had no time for brand names (oh, for a pair of Guess? jeans), but I usually came home with at least a new sweater and a pair of off-brand jeans that I would plan to wear on the first day of school. September still feels like summer in Chicago, a fact I steadfastly refused to accept throughout my childhood. The first day of school would invariably dawn sunny and 85 degrees. No matter. Unwilling to relinquish the outfit I had envisioned, I would stand at the bus stop, sweaty and uncomfortable in my new sweater.

In skipping our regular end-of-summer outing to the outlet malls this year, I have found myself wondering how this custom of new school clothes ever came to be in the first place. I have wondered if the origins of back to school shopping might date

back to the days when uniforms were more prevalent. My Cath-
olic school-educated father never tired of telling us how each
year he received only one pair of pants and two shirts for school.
Upon returning from school he had to hang up the shirt and
pants, and change into "play clothes" so that his uniform would
last the duration of the school year. I don't think he was exagger-
ating. I have seen springtime childhood photos of both my father
and his brother (who eventually topped out at six-foot-eight)
with their school pants well above their ankles.

For my father, and likely lots of other young Catholics from
the 1940 and 50s, the start of the school year was a natural moment for acquisition. Old items were worn through or ill-fitting,
and school attire had an expected formality. There was an actual
need for new clothes. Come September, however, my own children have plenty of clothes that still fit, are suitable for school,
and have lots of wear still left in them. If school weren't starting
next week, no one would be asking me about the state of Oliver's
wardrobe.

In the same way that a ten-week summer vacation is no
longer a necessity, but rather a vestige of our agrarian past, I
am beginning to think the notion of "new school clothes" might
be, too. Not so much of our agrarian past, but of a time when
school clothes were fewer and more formal. Despite this no longer being the case, now that the idea has taken root, much like
summer vacation, entire cultural norms have been built around
it. A quick late-August tour of major retail websites – The Gap,
Old Navy, Land's End – reveals back-to-school sales at each
featuring "hot deals" and "latest trends." Message received. I am
supposed to be getting my boys some new clothes.

I'd like to think this phenomenon is at the root of my previous belief that Oliver and my other two need new school clothes.
It would be comforting to imagine that I have simply fallen prey
to the manipulative forces of advertising; that I have been swept
up in the cultural tide of back to school sales, and just need to

get my wits about me. But I am pretty certain there is something else going on. My heretofore unexamined commitment to getting Oliver some new clothes *might* reflect the fact that I believe his high school success – social, academic, or otherwise – is related to how he looks or, more accurately, what he owns. There is a part of me – likely the same part of me determined to don a sweater on a hot September first – that thinks nice, new clothes say something about who we are.

Oh, what a sentence to put down in print. We all know better than to judge books by their covers. Yet, where would the fashion industry be if it didn't contain some kernel of truth? Who among us hasn't felt more confident in a great outfit? There are real psychological benefits to liking the way we are dressed. In the best-case scenario, our clothes allow us to express something essential about ourselves.

And so, after some consideration, the presenting parental question for me had to shift. It is no longer whether or not to buy Oliver new school clothes, but instead: what can Oliver choose to say about himself with the clothes he already has?

If Oliver were tasked with putting together an outfit that really captures him, my guess is that he'd wear the dancing bear hoodie he recently purchased this summer at a head shop. Oliver has long been a fan of classic rock, but he has only just discovered The Dead. The dulcet tones of Jerry Garcia formed the soundtrack to the last weeks of summer at our house.

I think he would pair this navy sweatshirt with his preferred pair of grey shorts, one of his few pairs that feels long enough to him. As a fellow tall person, I get this. Items that hit normal-heighted people in normal places are just slightly off for us. There's always too much of us sticking out somewhere. So when we find the rare item that runs a little long, we seize on our chance to look, and therefore feel, just like everyone else.

Isn't this what we all want out of our clothing – to telegraph that we are just like everyone else, and yet simultaneously, our own beautiful selves? This combination may, in fact, lie at the root of that subjective and wonderful experience of what it feels like to "look good." And if so, surely nothing could give more lie to the notion that we need to acquire the same new jeans, from the same stores, at the same time that everyone else does. My clothes do their best work for me when they fit me so well that I can think beyond them, and when – at the same time – they hint at what's special about me, without me having to say a thing. When they are both familiar and distinct.

If one were to use this standard for evaluating a wardrobe, it would still allow for the purchase of new items. In fact, currency is almost implied. For clothes to fit I need things that work on the body I currently have, plus or minus the five pounds that I may or may not be carrying. We also need clothes that reflect both fashion trends and our changing preferences, Grateful Dead or otherwise.

But if currency is implied, so is specificity. And this, at last, may be the change I am beginning to make. Between the ease of online shopping, and the relative affordability of regular discount shopping, it is possible to quickly acquire a LOT of clothes. A recent article in *The Atlantic* noted that, on average, Americans purchase 66 new items of clothing per person, per year. In 2015, we put *16 million tons* of textiles in municipal waste streams. That's the behavior I need to change. Filling my family's closets with clothing we only sort-of love means we're not just buying cheap goods that will end up in the waste stream, we are failing to scratch the itch that led us to buy clothes in the first place. We aren't purchasing clothes that make us feel great because they are distinctly us. Because they fit, in every sense of the word.

Fewer outfits comprised of clothes I love. On repeat. That's my new mantra. As for Oliver, well, it turns out I wasn't far off. He wore the gray shorts but forewent the sweatshirt. It was 90-degrees here on the first day of school.

THE LIBRARY

My public library has a social worker, falcons that nest on the roof ledge, and a teen loft frequented by my son and his friends on rainy afternoons. It has studious college kids, job seekers, and a cascading three-story mobile hung from the ceiling in the central stairway. There's a nature soundtrack that plays in the children's room, and filters upstairs to provide patrons with occasional bouts of rushing water and birdsong. I love my library.

In a capitalist society, libraries are not self-evident. "When you think about it... a public library is a really strange idea," writes children's author Linda Sue Park. "You walk in, you get yourself an armful of books and you walk out without paying a cent." Park's father, a Korean immigrant unable to get over the free bounty of the library, insisted that her family become members. To this day, one can find Park at the library at least twice a week.

No other item, aside from books, exists in free circulation for use by citizens and supported by government funds. Viewed in this light, the library and its resources can seem downright socialist. And yet, the public library movement was given its most important push forward by steel magnate and capitalist icon, Andrew Carnegie, a man whose driving philanthropic mission was to "help those who help themselves." Carnegie believed that access to public libraries, and the knowledge contained therein, were an essential first rung on the ladders people climb out of poverty.

For a long period of my life, I forgot libraries existed. The story of my engagement, falling away, and eventual return, I now realize, mirrors my relationship to church. Both began with parent-mandated participation that gradually waned, only to come full-circle with a kind of prodigal daughter return. Library-going was instilled in me as a young child, though it was not an entirely high-minded habit. My childhood home had no central air conditioning. Seeking some (free) relief from the humid Midwestern summer, my mother would load my sister and me into our station wagon and drive us to the library for the films that played there on Friday mornings. I was always happy with this trip, happy to spend post-film hours browsing the shelves, and happier still to sit down in the cool of the library's reading room and do nothing but read.

I remained loyal to the library throughout high school and into college, where it took on another dimension for me, functioning as a sort of social hub for the bookish. Trips to the library in college were a relief from the claustrophobia of the long Northeastern winters. I loved bundling up and heading out, entering the bright warmth of the library, and eventually settling into a carrel with my Nalgene water bottle, an apple, and my stacks of books and notes. Equally, I loved the breaks to stand, stretch, and take a few laps around the place to see who else happened to be there. In the days before social media served to connect us, these serendipitous interactions drew me out.

During my urban-dwelling twenties, I stopped using the library. Still pre-Amazon, my need for books was met by bookstores that, as a bonus, were a place to meet a date for coffee, with far better amenities and ambiance than the library. This hiatus from the library continued for over a decade, until I had kids of my own, and remembered that libraries are among the

few public spaces that actually *welcome* small children. During
my sons' early years we became Children's Department regulars,
attending read-aloud story time, crafting, and participating in
summer reading challenges. I realize now, however, that during
none of these visits did it occur to me that the giant rest of the
library was there for me, as an adult, to use, too.

↜↝↞

A few years ago I re-entered the library on my own. I had been
asked to conduct a focus group on behalf of a local philanthropy,
and looking for a neutral and accessible location to hold the conversation, I landed on the Waukegan Public Library. The town
of Waukegan hugs the shore of Lake Michigan, some 35 miles
north of Chicago. Like many rust belt towns, its situation is made
complex by environmental hazards, white flight, and significant
poverty. The heart of Waukegan is as close to the lake as that of
my own hometown, which manages to parlay this proximity into
astronomical rents and real estate prices. Not so, Waukegan.

The purpose of the focus group was to better understand
barriers to healthcare access for low-income residents. Over
the course of the conversation, participants passed along their
shared knowledge, relaying a series of horrific encounters with
the health care system. A woman with a postage stamp of gauze
taped over her right eye revealed that the doctors had recently
"taken" her eye. "I had a stye the size of a grape," she told me.
"My eyelid fell apart like a piece of wet paper." Another man,
with a gap where his front teeth should have been, registered his
complaints with the free local dental care. An older white woman
named Marge, bunions bulging from the slides of her sandals,
complained that her feet hurt so badly it was hard for her to
get out to see her doctor. She wondered aloud if visiting nurses
could come to her home instead. "Nah," shared an elderly black
man named Freddie, "they discontinued that program years

ago." Someone asked when. "Not sure," he said with a wry smile, "but I think it was right about the time they built the jail."

❧

Social services and the library intersect everywhere today. In the closing chapters of *The Library Book*, her love letter to librar- ies, Susan Orlean details the Los Angeles Public Library's effort to host a central "hub" of all LA's social services, so that those availing themselves of multiple kinds of assistance could make only one stop. Those in charge of the event were thrilled with the turnout, ecstatic that people were ready, willing, and able to come to the library for human services. In fact, as the library staff suspected, many of the intended beneficiaries were already there. So big was the assembled crowd, that Orlean herself is pressed into service filling out intake forms for those in line.

One explanation for modern libraries' bent toward service provision is their very "publicness" and accessibility. As Orlean observes, "It becomes harder all the time to think of places that welcome everyone and don't charge any money for that warm embrace." She goes on to explain that "the commitment to inclu- sion is so powerful that many decisions about the library hinge on whether or not a particular choice would cause a subset of the public to feel uninvited." A public library's doors, by definition, must remain open to all.

As true as this may be, something else must be pressing libraries into the realm of human service. After all, it would be possible to passively receive an entire citizenry and remain on mission, providing access only to the knowledge found online and in books. Libraries are not restricting themselves in this way. In towns both rural and urban, they are offering literacy training and job readiness classes, after school programs and translation services. They have pushed far beyond information provision and into the realm of active support.

Libraries and churches have more in common than my lifelong pattern of use. Both institutions, at their best, are spaces absent consumerism. Their contents and services are offered entirely free of entry fee or charge. Consumption-free space has a subtle alchemy that alters everything within it; books, a commodity in other settings, are decommodified at the library, becoming instead a communal resource. People, too, come to matter in a different way. Mary McCoy, a librarian featured in Orlean's book, attempts to explain some impromptu help provided by library staff to an undocumented teen: "It's a fine line... sometimes you act on your conscience. All the department librarians chipped in and bought her a bus pass and little things to help her." In a space free of consuming, our behavior can take a turn for the unexpected.

✄✁

A few weeks ago I sat writing at a different library, an extremely small one, located at the heart of a wealthy North Shore suburb just south of Waukegan. I set up my laptop on a table in the reading room and left in search of books. When I returned with an armful, an older lady in workout clothes and a pair of glasses with bright blue frames was seated at my table reading the large print edition of *When Life Gives You LuluLemons*. "Hello," she whispered as I placed my books on the table and took my seat. "I hope it's warmer in here. They have the air conditioning in the reading room up way too high." She continued. "Have you read this book?" she said, holding up her copy, "It's good. It's really funny. Do you think it's cold over here?"

It went on like this, intermittently, for the next hour or so. In the course of chatting, I learned that she comes to the library to read because her condo neighbors make too much noise during the day. I learned that she earned a B.A. from a college for teachers but went into financial planning instead. I answered questions about my children and the writing I was doing. At one point, I lent her the cardigan that I had brought with me, as she was still cold. When she finally got up to leave, she talked to me for another 10 minutes about her noisy neighbors, folding, smoothing, and refolding my cardigan as she spoke. Finally, she handed me my folded sweater and said, "Well, have a good day. And," she added, apropos of nothing we had been talking about, "be careful when you park at the beach."

Nowhere else could I imagine myself handing over my clothing to a complete stranger. The entire interaction could only have occurred in the library; my behavior was an extension of the institution in which I found myself. In creating and preserving a non-transactional space – an environment free of buying and selling – libraries are protecting a different kind of world; one that counters our increasing tendency to commodify one another, and allows, instead, our basic humanity to come to the fore. Contrast this environment to that of the healthcare system as described by my focus group attendees, people so completely commodified by that system that they had become cynical enough to see it. "The doctors don't call you to follow-up on your tests or appointments," observed Freddie during that conversation, "but somehow they manage to find you when the bills are due." In a place like the library, people are neither buyer nor seller – nor, most importantly, product.

MEDITATION ON PLENTY

L ate last night, in a cul-de-sac at the end of a terminal in the Philadelphia International Airport, after many "on-time departures" had blown away in gusts of 60-mile-an-hour winds, I stood in line waiting to board the second-to-last Southwest flight bound for Chicago.

For those not familiar with Southwest's boarding process, it involves using a letter (A-C) and a number (1-60) on your boarding pass to line up accordingly. Southwest does not designate specific seats for specific passengers. The idea is that the lower your letter and number, the greater your choice of seat. A1-A60 is likely to get the aisle or window they prefer; C1-C30, far more likely to get stuck in a middle seat toward the back of the plane.

The number on your boarding pass is not randomly assigned. Online check-in opens 24- hours prior to the flight, and the sooner you check in, the better your number. Back in the day, when the process first started, it was a straight meritocracy; early birds got their A1 worms. But like any good meritocracy rooted in a capitalist context, over time, the system has been corrupted. It is now possible to purchase literal "Early Bird" privileges, meaning that regardless of when you check in during the 24-hour period, if you have paid the early bird fee, you magically get an A assignment. Go figure.

My favorite part about the whole boarding routine is the actual lining up. The process is one-part honor system and one-part ice-breaker. It reminds me of those team-building games in which participants are instructed to line up by birth order without speaking to one another. Once the gate agent announces over the squawking P.A. system that it's time to board, all you can really do is stand approximately where you think you belong in line, and hope that those falling in around you are doing the same.

One would assume that a Type A personality (also likely to have an A-assignment) would feverishly and obsessively check to ensure that those around her are lining up in the correct order – that we are all getting what we deserve. In my experience, however, the process seems to produce the opposite effect. Everyone exhibits a polite nonchalance, feigned though it may sometimes be. As the gate agent calls out the numbers, there ensues an embarrassed, half-hearted checking to make sure you haven't inadvertently cut the line, yet not once have I encountered someone concerned or angry enough to insist they board in front of their neighbor with a similar number. More often, I see B21 happy to let B22 go ahead despite the mix up. Friendly shrugs and "doesn't really matter..." become refrains of the line.

We behave this way, I believe, because we are boarding the plane with a sense of plenty. Each of us in line knows that we have a seat on the plane. No one is getting left behind. Maybe we will end up in a middle seat, but by the time boarding is over, we'll all be watching the safety presentation together as we taxi toward the runway.

In a context of plenty, we can afford to be kind.

≪✧≫

Plenty is a funny word. Used one way, it indicates an overabundance, as in land of plenty or plenty of fish in the sea. Picture here someone with arms turned upward and spread wide, as if to say, *Look at all we have. There is so much as to be ridiculous or redundant. Help yourself.*

Employed in a different way, plenty connotes something closer to just enough, suggesting that a person with plenty has exactly what they need to get the job done. My grandfather, when offered dessert, would often push back from the table protesting, "No, thank you. I've had an elegant sufficiency." This phrase seems to me to capture the essence of this other kind of plenty, the one in which needs have been beautifully, almost perfectly, met. This version of plenty also seems to suggest a natural and appropriate stopping point; the speaker's gesture here is hands extended, palms facing forward, as if to halt the oncoming of more.

While a precise definition of plenty may be elusive, our search for it is pervasive. We are always trying to understand how much is enough, and how much, therefore, is more than enough. The question surfaces everywhere, from issues of national policy – how many and what types of immigrants do we allow across our borders, at what rate should we tax the very wealthy? to minor family drama – how often does she expect us to call, how many times should we bail him out?

I sometimes wonder if we prefer to fixate on the question of plenty because it begs the deeper, harder question at the heart of the matter. By focusing on the secondary issue of how much, we are exempt from examining the initial premise. Should our country's borders be open? Are we enabling our loved one?

 презентация

"I know what it is to be in need, and I know what it is to have plenty," the Apostle Paul writes to the church in Philippi. "I have learned the secret of being content in any and every situation, whether well-fed or hungry, whether living in plenty or in want."

Confession: I've been reading Philippians all wrong. Here's the way the text reads in my mind: *I have known what it is to have plenty. (And believe me that is GREAT.) But then things went wrong and, well, I have known what it is to have need. But I somehow manage to still be content, even during the lean times when I am living in want.*

See what I did there? How quickly I equated contentment with times of plenty? As though the writer's real feat was finding a way to be happy only when he was without. As though the lesson is to buck up when we are in need, muddling through until we get back to plenty again. My interpretation isn't supported by the text. The passage does not link contentment to plenty. Read closely and you'll see the challenge of the contentment posed equally to both the haves and have-nots.

Contentment dances around the same sense of fullness that plenty evokes. But while plenty's formal definition appears strictly quantifiable (*n. – a situation in which food and other necessities are available in sufficiently large quantities*), contentment has another dimension. Its formal definition includes phrases like "satisfaction" and "state of peaceful happiness." Contentment is not about physical well-being, it's about the condition of our soul.

The distinction is easy enough to grasp, but much harder to hold on to. Dwell too long in a culture of consumerism, and the relationship between plenty and contentment begins to blur. We're after a sense of fulfillment, but are relentlessly driven towards excess. And once we get to this point – of satiation, of engorgement – it becomes difficult to remember the need we were trying to fill in the first place.

ৎৎৡৡ

I have thought a lot this year about the notion of plenty. For an objective concept – resources sufficient to the situation at hand

– it remains stubbornly subjective. And the fear that, by some operating definition of the word, there may not be "enough" calls out the worst parts of human nature. It pushes us toward demarcation and division; we draw lines around what is ours to hold on to it. We look with suspicion at those approaching.

Understood in a societal context, plenty should then imply the opposite; that we are free to want for others what we want for ourselves. It seems easy, but this is, in fact, a hard-won freedom. It requires not only holding fast to our own sense of abundance, but also an ability to see the other and to acknowledge the basic truth that our lives are, in fact, connected.

Nowhere is this truth more evident than among a group of passengers waiting to board a plane. Last night when a slight man with thick glasses turned around to make sure he was in the right spot in line, he discovered he was mistakenly in front of his neighbor. As he hurried to move out of the way, this neighbor, a dapper, older man with salt and pepper hair and a tan trench coat hung over his arm, gestured for the man to move back in front of him. "It's all right," he said with a chuckle, "we're all gonna end up in the same place."

෴

What would the world look like if everyone knew with assurance that there was enough for them? How might we behave if forced to acknowledge that our fates are linked and we are all going to end up in the same place? My experience in the boarding line suggests it would lower our anxiety and reduce our need for status symbols. We might begin to see our neighbors in a new light, and find ourselves surprisingly inclined to put their needs ahead of our own.

But to do this, to really stop competing with one another, we would need to change the conditions. Rather than inhabit a universe of perceived scarcity, those of us with plenty would

need to live as though there was enough. I would need to let go
of the fear that just because you got yours doesn't mean that I
am in danger of losing mine. I would need to let go of the fear of
you.

Airports are places that change the conditions. In gate areas
and security lines, we are a people connected, subject to weather,
regulation, and forces beyond our control. Poet Naomi Shihab
Nye understands the potential here. In her poem, *Gate A4,* she
relates the story of an elderly Palestinian woman and a group
of strangers at an airline gate. Distraught because she does not
speak English, and cannot understand why her flight has not left,
the elderly woman has collapsed in tears in front of a bewildered
gate agent. Nye comes to the woman's aid, offering translation
and, thereby, consolation. Over the course of the poem, other
passengers at the gate are drawn into her story until a community is formed. Together they talk and laugh. Eventually the passengers receive the elderly woman's date cookies and some free
airline apple juice, Nye tells us,"like a sacrament."

"Not a single person in that gate – once the crying of confusion stopped – seemed apprehensive about any other person,"
she observes. "They took the cookies. I wanted to hug all those
other women, too." In the last lines of the poem, Nye claims
hope. "This can still happen anywhere," she tells us of her gate
experience. "All is not lost."

Each time I reach the climax of this poem, I get goose-
bumps. I want to cheer and embrace Nye's vision of a "shared
world," but I am cautious, skeptical about my own capacities,
doubtful of others'. Where I live, despite demonstrable plenty,
mindsets of scarcity and individualism carry the day. Contentment is elusive. The scene at the gate feels like the exception and
not the rule.

Ah, but the mistake is mine; again I'm reading the text all
wrong. I'm trying to take a poem literally. I'll start at the beginning, and this time I'll stay with the metaphor. Only when I step

back will I see what Nye has been trying to tell me all along: in spaces where we are connected, in places of plenty – it is there that we take flight.

THE PEOPLE WE LOVE REMAIN

Ask me about the best gift I ever received, and I'd have difficulty answering. One year John made me a cookbook holder with hinges and a Plexiglas cover to protect the pages from splatter while I cooked. I loved that.

Gifts from my children are precious. One of my recent favorites was a book: Zadie Smith's collection of essays, *Changing My Mind*. The gift came from my 14-year-old. I think he was hoping I would take the title as suggestion.

But the gift that comes to mind for me as the best gift, was given to me by my father. He gave it to me when I was a junior in high school, though I can't remember for what occasion. Perhaps, like all the best gifts, there was no particular occasion. The gift was a set of vocabulary flash cards initially purchased many years ago for his own edification. The cards contained "challenging" words of the type I was attempting to memorize at the time for my upcoming SAT exam. Each card featured the vocabulary word front and center in a basic 1960s font: *lugubrious*, *pernicious*, *gregarious*, with the definition found on the flip side. The cards were packed in their original, faded box which had started out navy and yellow, but was now white at the corners, in the manner of all aged and distressed cardboard.

I don't think the gift came wrapped. As I recall, my father

simply brought it into my room, sat down on my bed, explained that the cards had been his, that he had kept and used them, and that he wanted now to pass them on to me. I loved them immediately. I loved the fact that the cards were not new; I see now that I have always had an affinity for objects that come seasoned, bearing stories of their own. The cards also captured something of my father's essence. They represented his abiding curiosity and intellect, his deep faith in the power of education, his commitment to a self-directed, lifelong scholarship. These are among the things I loved most about him.

The gift wasn't just a way of knowing my father. The vocabulary cards were also evidence that my father knew *me*. It was as though he understood that by giving me words, I would know exactly what to do with them. Turns out, he was right. I've been playing with them ever since.

≈৩≈

Christmas launches gift season at our house, which continues right through two early January birthdays. Perhaps it goes without saying that for us, gift season has become synonymous with excess. While hardly an excuse, it doesn't help that these events – Christmas, birthdays – coincide with winter in Chicago. Anyone who has lived through a Chicago winter knows it as an exercise in sensory deprivation. Sounds are muffled by hats and earmuffs, drowned out by the sloshing of passing cars. Cold-numbed fingers make touch an impossibility. Stuffed and runny noses block out even the best odors, and eagerness to dive into mugs of hot coffee or chocolate results in scalded, useless tongues. The worst offense, however, is what the winter does to sight. Frost and mud conspire everywhere to deprive the landscape of color. A dull brown-gray, exactly the color you'd get from months of mixing cold with dirt, dominates in a monotone universe.

The colorful excess of the holidays makes some sense against this backdrop. Holiday gift-giving restores joy to an otherwise cold and barren landscape. I have often wondered, frankly, why people in Florida or California need Christmas at all. Close your eyes for a moment, and picture a toy store, bookstore, or boutique. Think of all the color and texture. Imagine coming out of the cold and dark into the warm light of these places, searching through the inventory, and bringing home the perfect gift for the people we love.

Although it can start innocently, it's amazing how quickly gift-giving escalates from a token of shared joy to an avalanche of stuff. How, before you know it, rather than reflecting the wants and needs of their intended receiver, the gifts become a kind of tautology, referencing only their own logic. New game console? New controllers required. New brown belt? Maybe a new pair of pants to wear it with. New phone? Here, open this gift! It contains your new phone case.

❧

In 1996 my father died in a plane crash, an event that, for a time, robbed me of faith in everything from God to gravity, and left a searing grief in its place. This white-hot grief, over time, has reduced to embers, which my children, occasionally and unknowingly, stoke. It is odd and more than a little sad to me that my boys will only ever know a concrete version of my father through his things – an old, olive green jacket from his brief stint in the Army; a small, bronze nameplate taken from the office he occupied as a young White House staffer; a brown pipe, the relic of a 1970s craze. To this day, the scent of tobacco smoke transports me to summer evenings, the hum of cicadas droning in through the open windows, my father, home from work and now in his comfy clothes, relaxing with his pipe in his large, brown chair.

Taken out of the context of a life, I worry that these items could be misunderstood; that they will lead my children to misinterpret him. My father didn't love his time in the service. He enlisted out of respect to his own father, a Purple Heart and Bronze Star decorated WWII vet, and a certainty that he would otherwise be drafted and sent to fight in Vietnam. The Washington D.C. he labored in does not resemble the current political environment in any meaningful way. As he aged, he gave up pipe smoking (and, unbelievably, coffee) for the pleasures of herbal tea and various attempts at gardening.

The trick, I am discovering, is to curate a collage of things that represent his life. Letters he wrote to me in college, books from his vast library, Ella Fitzgerald on vinyl. Adding these items to the mix gets me closer, but I am still uneasy.

At some point it will be left to someone else to tell our story, and they'll have to work with the props that we leave them. It is through our objects that, in large part, we will be known. But objects alone are insufficient to the job of communicating a life. They need the connective tissue of story and people. We are truly understood – fully animated – only in relationship to one another.

∽∾

In O. Henry's Christmas story, *The Gift of the Magi*, the two main characters, a poor married couple, famously sacrifice their dearest possessions to buy gifts for one another, only to have their loving act result in futility. Della, observing how much her husband cherishes his gold watch, sells her hair to purchase a watch chain for him. And Jim, knowing how Della covets a set of jeweled combs for her hair, sells his watch to get her the combs.

O. Henry's tale has always devastated me. Even in the above summarizing I was made sad. Reading it, for me, is a bit like watching a horror movie; knowing something terrible is about to occur, but by virtue of watching (or, in this case, reading) rendered unable to prevent it. "No!" I want to yell to Della as she enters Mme. Sofronie's shop for Hair Articles of all Kinds. "Don't do it!"

What is it about this story that keeps us coming back? My first hunch was that we're hooked on the sick irony of the thing, but upon a recent read I am more certain it is the redemptive end. As the narrative portion of the story comes to a climax, the fateful error about to be revealed, Jim says with a smile, "Dell... let's put our Christmas presents away and keep 'em awhile. They are too nice to use just at present." He continues, plowing on with the bad news, "I sold the watch to get the money to buy your combs." And then, without even giving us a glimpse into Della's reaction, O. Henry plows on with more from Jim. "Now suppose you put the chops on." Fade to black.

At this point, we get no more plot or dialogue, only reflection from our omniscient narrator helping us make sense of what has just happened. It is as though O. Henry doesn't want any additional action to distract us from the point he is trying to make: despite their ill- fated decisions, Jim and Della are wise givers. They are, the narrator explains, "like the magi," the wise men who brought gifts to the Christ child. Their gifts are so painfully perfect, the characters' understanding of one another so complete, that the material goods cancel themselves out. In the face of love like this, actual items become obsolete. All that's left is the act of giving and the knowledge of the other.

෨෩

On Christmas morning, when I was a child, my sister and I would wait at the top of the stairs while my father went down first to "see if Santa had come." As he built a fire and made a pot of coffee, the two of us would sit on the top step, squirming in anticipation and calling down for a report about what he had seen. And while I can remember with clarity, the joy of bouncing on the step next to her, and the speed with which we rushed

down the stairs, for the most part I do not remember the gifts.
I can picture piles of wrapped presents, boxes clad in Santa's
wrapping paper (strategically unlike any other under the tree),
but aside from one beloved doll, I could not, for the life of me,
tell you what was in them.

This is the way it's supposed to go. Like the O. Henry story,
the material becomes immaterial, the people we love remain.
Not the other way around. The tragedy of my father's death and
the mark of his absence transform a box of vocabulary cards into
something much more valuable.

≪≫

Christmas will soon be here at our house again. How we will
respond to our annual exercise in excess remains at issue. For
some reason, abandoning the tradition of birthday or Christmas gifts doesn't sit well with any of us, even though none of
us has, at the moment, a burning desire for any one particular
item. Still, to give a gift, we feel, is to acknowledge the other.
Foregoing one would amount to disregard.

So, how to give well in the face of neither need nor want?
How to find something that communicates to those I love that
they are seen? That they are known? The answer, I think, lies
in the distinction between living through our things, yet not for
them. Our gifts serve us best when they connect us but do not
overtake us.

To give in this way, O. Henry instructs, we must first give
of ourselves, and to each other so thoroughly that the material
melts away. Della and Jim paid attention. Likewise, I have to be
paying attention to what makes my boys laugh and what they are
curious about. What childhood favorite they are still really into,
despite their protestations to the contrary, and what unexplored
frontiers of adulthood are currently piquing their interest. Only
then will I land on the very thing that, ironically, doesn't matter

at all. Some token that will eventually be forgotten or lost or left behind in a move but will signal to my boys that, at this moment, I see them. That they are known and loved, as my father knew and loved me. "Of all who give and receive gifts," O. Henry tells us, "such as they are the wisest."

MUDDYING WALDEN

"Total phony." So declared my mom the first time I asked her about Henry David Thoreau and his Walden Pond retreat. "You know what?" she continued with disdain, "the whole time he claimed to be living alone in the woods he was walking over to the Emersons' house for dinner. And [here pausing for an indignant sniff] his mother used to bring him cookies." With that last bit of evidence, she rested her case and returned to making dinner.

I am sure I took my mother's literary critique with a grain of salt. My mom, while a great reader, is a contrarian, often looking to take up the unpopular part, especially where books are concerned. (Her read on Fitzgerald's *Great Gatsby*? "It's okay. I just don't get what he saw in Daisy.") I am certain I heard this take on Thoreau as her typical caution not to get infatuated with someone or something due to popular sentiment. It's possible I may have placed my high school loaner copy of *Walden* prominently on my nightstand a few days after hearing it, without ever having read a page of the book. Such was my sort of stab at teenage rebellion.

Occasionally, this tendency of my mother's lands her on the right side of history. These days it is difficult to find a pro-Thoreau review that doesn't first run through a litany of disclaimers and qualifiers of the kind that Kathryn Schulz offers up in her

2015 New Yorker article, "Pond Scum: Henry David Thoreau's Moral Myopia." Schulz's read on Thoreau seems hard to repudiate. Her essay is thick with objectionable Thoreau quotes, revealing a hypocritical and judgmental writer full of contempt for his fellow human beings. His certainty in his own principles, coupled with an apparent lack of curiosity about the other, makes for a man who had, as Schulz describes, an "antipathy toward humanity [that] encompassed the very idea of civilization."

Schulz's piece gave me pause. I had reread *Walden* a few weeks prior, as I thought he might have something to say to me about our family's commitment to eschew consumer culture and strive for self-reliance (albeit with the aid of indoor plumbing and the thousands of goods we already owned). Sure, we weren't making our clothes or furniture, but nor were we purchasing things, "led by the love of novelty and regard for the opinions of men." Like Thoreau, we were trying to operate from a standpoint of "true utility." I felt, in preparing to reread him, like I might encounter a kindred spirit.

My copy of *Walden* suited its content. The book, a tattered gray paperback, had been my father's. Another prolific reader, my father left behind a large library of used books, mostly paperbacks with yellowed pages, incredibly small fonts, and a musty bookish smell. Many of them still carried their original or used bookstore price tags. From a gold oval price tag affixed to the cover of his copy, it would appear that my father purchased *Walden* for $1.25. If that was the original tag, left in place to show the used book shopper what a good deal he was getting, then it is possible my father got the book for less. Thoreau, I think, would have been proud.

Much to my disappointment, my father made no notes in his copy of *Walden*, save for some cryptic marks with a faded felt tip pen inside the front cover denoting what appears to be a phone number. I am not sure how to read the lack of any other notation by a man who regularly marked up his texts with penciled-in questions in an unmistakable angular script. Did my father grow weary of Thoreau's self-righteousness? Did he end up skimming "Economy," the first section of the book, and begin reading in earnest at, "Where I Lived, and What I Lived For"?

I did both those things: grew weary of Thoreau, and still managed to follow him into the woods. And I'm glad I did. Because as even Schulz will admit, to read Thoreau on life in the woods is to read some of the best nature writing around. Here he is on the display of autumn maples near his house: "Already, by the first of September, I had seen two or three small maples turned scarlet across the pond... Ah! Many a tale their color told. And gradually from week to week the character of each tree came out, and admired itself reflected in the smooth mirror of the lake. Each morning the manager of this gallery substituted some new picture, distinguished by more brilliant or harmonious col- oring, for the old upon the walls." This particular passage got a little starred pencil mark from me.

But it is with no small degree of sheepishness, that I am also here to report starring passages in "Economy." And underlining them. And even, I feel compelled to admit, inserting the random exclamation point in the margins, which, in my own glossary of notations, signifies total agreement. For despite all the problematic commentary on his fellow man, Thoreau was making observations that resonated with me. He was describing the very trap our family had fallen into, calling out the way our stuff required the acquisition of additional stuff, and, more importantly, a commitment of our time and resources. "When I consider how our houses are built and paid for, or not paid for, and their eternal economy managed and sustained," he observes, "I wonder that the floor does not give way under the visitor while he is admiring the gew-gaws upon the mantelpiece."

My notations continue as Thoreau links our misguided fascination with acquisition and luxury to modern technology. He seems prescient when he comments, "So with a hundred 'modern improvements;' there is an illusion about them; there is not always positive advance... Our inventions are wont to be pretty toys, which distract our attention from serious things. They are but improved means to an unimproved end..." I have yet to find a better description of the smartphone anywhere.

So when Schulz excoriated Thoreau, I guess I felt convicted as well. I began to see myself as a similarly privileged buffoon, playing at minimalism while going to my mom's for cookies. Schulz wasn't wrong about us – HDT and me – and the more I returned to her article, the more I cringed. And yet, there were some differences that gave me hope. Our year of no buying had not removed us from the company of others. Unlike Thoreau, I like people. I had no urge to get away from them. Moreover, as any good citizen living in the "you do you" era, I had no strong feelings about the behavior of others, consuming or otherwise. It ws your business if Amazon dropped packages on your doorstep every day. Not only did I feel no judgment about the shopping habits of my family and friends, the entire exercise of not buying was growing my affection for the people in my life, mostly by virtue of the time I was now able to spend with them.

Thoreau and I may have been of one accord on the problem of material excess, but we could not be farther apart on the solution. Thoreau's response to being caught in the "spider's web" of our things is to cut all the ties that bind. Every last one of them. He isn't just seeking distance from the trappings of modern life, but from the society of man that promotes them. For Thoreau, if the source of the problem is keeping up with the Joneses, best to get as far away from the Joneses as possible. Only at a distance from the quietly desperate mass of men can we begin to live in a way that honors both our existence and the planet.

This idea – that the best, purest life is the one we have when we go it alone – works when retreating to nature. It allows for close encounters with animals, detailed descriptions of flora, and quasipsychedelic visions brought on by extreme hunger and a summer rain. (See passage in which Thoreau, bathed in the light of a rainbow, fancies himself looking through a colored crystal and living "like a dolphin.") It also worked in 1845, when being alone in nature was still a possibility for much of the population. But I am not so sure it works now, in this time, on this crowded planet. With the majority of people alive today living in cities, and the long reach of the Internet, fulfilling Thoreau's prescription for solitude is a logistical nightmare.

More than that, however, I am convinced that Thoreau's brand of self-enforced solitude is wrong-headed. If this year of no buying has persuaded me of anything, it is that my every action is interrelated and intertwined with the lives of others. Where a thing is produced, who is producing it, where it will ultimately end up – all a matter of consequence. I often wish it were otherwise, but try as I might after this year, I can no longer ignore it.

To go off the grid, to separate ourselves and our decisions from the larger whole, is to avoid some of the pitfalls of modern life. But it is also to shirk some responsibility. When we exit fully the systems that surround us – market, government, or otherwise – we leave behind their flaws, but we also forfeit the chance to make them better. And while we may change things for ourselves, I worry that we fail to change things, in any meaningful way, for those who come after us.

⪍↭⪎

In her memoir, *The Dirty Life*, author and farmer Kristin Kimball, an Ivy League- educated, New York City-based writer, follows her boyfriend and soon-to-be husband, Mark, to a farm in upstate New York. Eager to distance himself from capitalism and its trappings, Mark "tried, as much as possible, to live outside the river of consumption that is normal life in America." Kimball goes on to explain, "He preferred secondhand everything, from underwear to appliances. Even better than secondhand was handmade. He dreamed aloud to me of someday making his own toothbrushes out of boars' bristles." If ever there was a latter-day Thoreau, Mark sounds like it. He even comes across as similarly frustrating on the page. Committed to elements of farm work that give *him* joy – hard work, connection to the land – Mark insists that the farm refrain from using milking machines and tractors. With seeming disregard for the toll this takes on those close to him, he instead requires Kristin and the other farm-hands to hand-milk cows and drive teams of Amish draft horses to plow the fields.

Where Mark and Thoreau diverge, however, is in their relationship to their community. While Thoreau is not entirely opposed to keeping company with others, his writing in *Walden* suggests that his interactions with his neighbors were episodic at best. And certainly, when it comes to dependence on these neighbors, Thoreau wanted no part of such entanglements. In *The Dirty Life*, on the other hand, the Kimballs seek them out. The vision driving their efforts is to produce a "whole diet" solution for up to 100 community members who might come to depend on their farm for everything from grain, to produce, to dairy, to meat. Over the course of the book, the Kimballs not only achieve the enviable position of provider, of being depended upon, but their story is also full of moments in which they take the role of the dependent. As young farmers new to their town, they make error after rookie error in their first year of farming. However, as word gets out that they are "serious" about their farm, long-time residents and fellow farmers begin to come to their aid – saving their tomato plants, helping them harvest their beans, lending them equipment – all the while having a good laugh at their expense.

No one said the company of others was easy.

❧

If Thoreau's retreat represents one response to the problems of modern society, and the Kimballs' another, I am left wondering where we fall with all this no buying. One central critique of our experiment, as leveled by more than a few people, is that we are withdrawing our cash from the local economy. Nowhere did we feel this more keenly than in the little upstate New York town we frequent each summer. The town is home to a general store of some renown, owned by the same family for over 50 years. Filled from scuffed wooden floor to tin ceiling with every item imaginable, it is an ideal place to meander on a rainy day, and a great place to pick up a book or a puzzle if more rain is in the forecast. It is also the only place in an approximately 50-mile radius to purchase basic home goods, anything from ice cube trays to curtain rods. So it is that every year we succumb to the tourist-priced hardware and housewares in the name of keeping money in the town versus the Walmart, located an hour away just off the Thruway. But during the year of no buying, while we did our part to keep our local ice cream stand in business, the general store got no support from us.

This kind of behavior, I fear, lands us in Thoreau territory. It puts the emphasis on withdrawal over connection, and individual over systems change. And when I weigh that against the kind of difference the Kimballs are making, I can't help but feel we come up short. If I believe that now, perhaps more than at any other time in history, my life and the choices that accompany it have implications for others, it's probably not enough for us to simply retreat from consumerism. We can't just opt out; we have to opt into something else instead.

Even after months of ruminating about the environment, our interconnectedness, and our material goods, I am not exactly sure what opting in means for me. I think it could look like environmental activism, or the decision to open our house to people in need. I suppose it could entail shopping exclusively at local independent merchants and farmers markets, or becoming active in movements like Freecycle or Buy Nothing that exist for the sole purpose of resource sharing outside the consumer economy. There is no shortage of options. What there is, I worry, is a shortage of will. Opting in, different than opting out, requires active attention and a dogged commitment to behavior change. I can't just go about my life, minus some shopping. I have to go about my life in a fundamentally different way.

I am writing the end of this essay in a funny little café in my hometown. I'm seated at a rickety table next to a nook, with a soft, blue armchair and a basket of used children's toys that are tacky to the touch. A few tables over, the café staff is having a meeting from which the manager just excused herself to meet her GED tutor who has just arrived. This café is a nonprofit culinary training site for young women who have dropped out of high school. It supports its staff with housing and other core services. Its bathrooms have posters about where to seek help if sexually assaulted. In the more public spaces of the café, the walls are painted a cheery yellow and filled with the works of local artists and some inspirational collage-style posters made by the program's participants promoting messages of strength and perseverance. Two tables over, a group of older women is playing mahjong and talking local school board politics.

It was raining when I came here today, so I decided to drive rather than bike or walk. When I backed my car out of the driveway, I discovered that my street was blocked by a tree trimming truck. The truck meant I had to make a left out of my driveway instead of a right. Which meant, in turn, that I passed this café before coming upon the Starbucks located two blocks away. And I stopped here, largely, because a parking space happened to open up just as I was passing by. No tree trimming truck or available parking spot? I would be at Starbucks right now.

What will we have gained if we finish the year with fewer possessions and no real behavior change? If choosing against consumption fails to progress from habit to instinct? Not much,

I'm afraid.

"Aim above morality," Thoreau famously exhorts a friend writing in search of guidance. "Be not simply good. Be good for something." This time he's right. I need to set my sights higher than winning the game we've created. I've got to find my something, and this may take some time. In the very same letter, immediately preceding this celebrated piece of advice, Thoreau offers more helpful, if less quotable, instruction. Be like a dog, he tells the young man, do what you love. "Know your own bone; gnaw at it, bury it, unearth it, and gnaw it still." Questions of consumption will continue to trouble me, but I will be patient. A year is hardly long enough. We will keep up the work of living with less; it will be the work of a lifetime.

EPILOGUE: PRIME DAYS

On March 13, 2020, my children were told to gather their essentials from their lockers and desks as the following day would be their last day of school for the month. This announcement was greeted with whoops of joy from my boys. Two weeks at home sounded like the mother of all snow days. They packed up, came home, and settled in.

One year later, they are still in our house, Zooming into class in their pajamas. While they go out sporadically, for the last 12 months their lives have largely centered here, in our home. Like any working parent writing to the future from this pandemic, I am compelled to report both good and bad. Dirty dishes litter our house. So do socks. No one seems to care much for matching them anymore; the sock situation seems headed toward entropy.

On the whole, however, finding our teenage boys back under our roof has been miraculous. We are getting an up-close look at their changes, hearing a first-hand account of the ways in which they are puzzling out life's bigger questions. Before the pandemic, these front-row seats were so often wasted on their friends. We, the parents, now have a much better view. After an intense discussion, confessional moment, or giant family comedy session, John and I often steal a glance at one another meant to communicate only one thing: "Can you believe this?"

Then there is our whole relationship to time. The massive slowing of our schedules, and the forced togetherness has distorted our sense of its passing. It's not uncommon for one of us to lose track of the day of the week. In this context, once small or mundane events – rehearsals, lessons, practices – have taken on grand significance. What a treat to get out of the house for some masked flag football or a trip to the grocery store.

A desire to slow down, to spend more time together – these were some of the most basic impulses behind our year of no buying. So I am left wondering just how it is that this time of slowing and togetherness has resulted in, of all things, more buying. Culturally, we are consuming at unprecedented rates. Analysis of e-commerce data shows a significant uptick in online shopping, not surprising given a public health crisis during which everyone is told to stay indoors. However, more general data from the National Retail Foundation shows that overall 2020 retail numbers were up .06% from last year, despite a floundering economy.

But my real proof that buying is on the rise? We, the Pratts, are buying again. We, the family of no buying. The one that took a year to clean and repurpose before purchasing. The same family that swore off fast fashion and unnecessary household goods. We, this family, have ordered hand towels for our downstairs bathroom and joined StitchFix. We got a new nonstick pan and threw out a shoddy charging station—despite some working ports in the old one)—replacing it with a better one. Over the course of the pandemic, we've acquired coffee mugs, dog beds, rain boots, books, a pizza peel, underwear, picture frames, a hand-held vacuum, noise-cancelling headphones, a new television, and a whole mess of face masks.

I can rationalize some of this. First, we are two years out from our year of no buying, and some of our items have become worn beyond repair, necessitating replacement. The new rain boots fall into this category, my old pair finally having cracked along the seam. Our ancient hand-held vacuum was no longer able to be jiggled or cajoled into further service. Even the new television can be explained, our eight-year-old set having blown a speaker at some point during last year's binge watching. It is possible, in the loosest sense of the word, that we needed some of what we bought.

In turn, the economy needed us. Or so we were told. Eat local, buy local. Think about what you want to see standing when this pandemic ends. Patronize neighborhood shops as an act of civic duty. Consume like your community depends on it. We heard these messages, and, good soldiers that we are, we went shopping.

But make no mistake about it, ours was not consumption as civic act. Our pandemic buying spree was foremost an exercise in distraction. We were among the pandemic's lucky ones; we stayed healthy and kept our jobs, allowed to work and learn from the confines of a comfortable home. But it is also true that we felt the creeping monotony of this reality, of living day in and day out in the same space, and we began to desire things to change it up, make it more beautiful. Hence the hand towels. We were also just bored and tempted, clicking around in our copious spare time. Hence a navy raincoat (you know, as long as I was getting the boots). Consuming during this bleak stretch felt great—something to produce a little dopamine and numb the omnipresent pain. When Amazon delivered a Spikeball set in July, well, Merry Christmas to us. We were all just trying to make it through.

How quickly we relinquished the habits of our experimental year: community, creativity, restraint, reuse! It's as though when the world caught fire, opting out of consumer culture was too much to ask. Yet everything I believed about consumption before the pandemic still holds true, now more than ever. Our earth is harmed by thoughtless buying. Socio-economic disparities are widened. And filling our homes with more stuff only temporarily relieves the anxiety and despair with which many of us live. In buying more, we're really just digging a deeper hole.

At some point during our pandemic lockdown, I discovered Prime Days at Amazon – the modern-day equivalent of a Kmart "Blue Light Special." Items across the e-commerce site were deeply discounted, and as we had once again become shoppers, I partook. The number of items in our cart grew each time I populated the search bar. I'm still not entirely sure how the essential oil diffuser found its way into my cart, except to say that Elliot was convinced his room smelled like feet and things must change. It would appear that we had come full circle. We were once again standard American consumers.

And yet.

John's 50th birthday fell a few months into lockdown. If ever there was an excuse to splurge, celebrating John was it. Latest Apple watch? New hiking boots? High-end exercise gear? It was all just a click away.

We closed the laptop and went a different route.

Years ago, after taking up a small brick patio and laying down a new one, the contractor asked if we'd like to keep the old bricks. Thick and made of clay, with a smooth purplish patina, the bricks are a thing of beauty. Where I saw rubble, John saw raw material and stacked them behind our garage. For years, the bricks remained there, serving a variety of needs from temporary fort construction to makeshift weights.

In the years since stacking the bricks, John has, when an aspirational mood strikes, entered "building brick pizza oven" in his search bar and watched the hundreds of resulting instructional YouTube videos. While quarantined, after watching yet another round of how-tos and still not taking action, despite having all the time in the world, he finally had to concede that he lacked the skill set to construct the oven. John's birthday present, we decided, would be an outsourcing of this long-delayed project. Nils, a handy neighbor, took it on using only mortar and insulation, some cinderblock and rebar, and our recycled bricks. A small igloo-shaped brick oven now stands outside our back door.

Everything about making pizza in your own, very-DIY pizza oven has a steep learning curve. Making pizza dough with the right consistency is an art, as is forming its springy mass into a round flat crust. Sliding the pizza off the peel, a long-handled oversized spatula designed for exactly this activity, requires technique. After that, timing is everything. We keep an eye on the oven ceiling as the flames lick across, and monitor the color shift from a dusty brown to charcoal black. Finally, when the ceiling is a blazing hot white, only then does John slide the pizzas in, shimmying the uncooked dough off the peel with a quick back-and-forth to deposit it on the oven floor.

Some nights have found all five of us clustered around the small oven door, fanning and blowing on a fledging fire. Cooking in our oven has required patience, and laughter, and a willingness to eat some pizza gone wrong. Hungry teenage boys are generous with their definition of "edible," ignoring undercooked dough or charred pepperoni in service of just starting to eat. Perhaps not surprising that when in the act of coaxing a pizza off the peel John or I accidentally folded it over on itself – a common occurrence in those early days – the boys saw not ruined pizza, but calzone.

Over time, we've gotten better. Friends have shown up with basil and tomatoes from their gardens and lent their dough-tossing expertise. Curious neighbors have wandered into the backyard, tempted by the twin odors of campfire and bread, and joined in the fire-tending. Pizzas now emerge steaming from the oven, evenly cooked. A final drizzle of olive oil and a sprinkling of sea salt has taken the whole thing over the top.

One day this winter, in the midst of a second surge of infection, and once again confined to our homes, I head outside to light a fire in the pizza oven. Standing outside, waiting for the larger logs to catch, I have an outsider's view of my home. Through the window, I see my boys at the kitchen table, laughing hard and pointing at the dog. My husband, standing at the counter, shakes his head in mock exasperation while rolling out dough. Flour coats more of the room than I care to think about. Woodsmoke blows out of the chimney as the cold air whips around me.

I am not sure we will ever be able to stop consuming. All evidence points to the fact that my family will continue to shop, despite a stated commitment to wanting less. But I'm no longer sure that not buying should ever have been the point. True, I wanted less stuff, but less was always just the means to a different end – a healthier planet, more time with family and friends, more justice, more community, more accidental calzones. What this year has made plain is that consumption is only one piece of the puzzle. While less shopping and less stuff is important, so is less stress, less scheduling, less screens. It's difficult to untangle; to know where to begin. Going forward, I wonder if we would be better served to start, instead, with what we want more of.

Hoots of laughter come from inside the house. Our black mutt, Gus, has nosed his way into the bag of flour sitting on the counter, and has overturned it on himself. He is running down the hall and Elliot is giving chase. Foster and Oliver are cheering them on. John punches and kneads pizza dough, ignoring the mayhem and mess, a skill we have perfected over the past year of constant togetherness. He looks up and meets my eyes through the window. Smiling, he shrugs and throws his dough-covered hands in the air. I know what he is trying to tell me because I feel it too: these are prime days.

⤜⤛

Works Referenced

Introduction
Patchett, Ann. "My Year of No Shopping." *New York Times.*
    15 December 2017.

Women's Work
Grose, Jessica. "Cleaning: The Final Feminist Frontier."
    The New Republic. 2013.
Hochschild, Arlie. *The Second Shift.* Viking Penguin, 1989.
Oliver, Mary. "I own a house." *Devotions: The Selected Poems
    of Mary Oliver.* Penguin Press, 2017.

Parsing Desire
Maslow, A.H. "A Theory of Human Motivation."
    Psychological Review, 1943.

All Consuming
Veblen, Thorstein. *The Theory of the Leisure Class.*
    Dover Publications, 1994.

Mine to Choose
Diamond, Jason. "Letter of Recommendation: Bialys."
    New York Times. 30 October 2018.
Schwartz, Barry. *The Paradox of Choice.*
    Harper Perennial, 2004.
Sunstein, Cass R. and Thaler, Richard H. *Nudge.*
    Yale University Press, 2008.

Oh Crap
Woloson, Wendy. *Crap: A History of Cheap Stuff in America.*
    University of Chicago Press, 2020.

Consider the Lobster
White, E.B. "Good-bye to Forty-Eighth Street." *Essays of E.B.
    White.* Harper Perennial, 1977.
Wallace, David Foster. "Consider the Lobster."
    Gourmet Magazine. August 2004.

PAYING ATTENTION
Odell, Jenny. *How to Do Nothing: Resisting the Attention Economy*. Melville House, 2020.

A FEW OF MY FAVORITE THINGS
Rosa, Hartmut. *Alienation and Acceleration*. NSU Press, 2010.

THE CUNNINGHAM GENE
Sherman, A., Grabowecky, M., and Suzuki, S. "In the working memory of the beholder: Art appreciation is enhanced when visual complexity is compatible with working memory." *Journal of Experimental Psychology: Human Perception and Performance*. 2015.

OUTFITTING OLIVER
Semuels, Alana. "We Are All Accumulating Mountains of Things." *The Atlantic*. 21 August 2018.

THE LIBRARY
Orleans, Susan. *The Library Book*. Simon & Schuster, 2018.

MEDITATION ON PLENTY
Nye, Naomi Shihab. "Gate A4." *Honeybee: Poems & Short Prose*. Greenwillow Books, 2008.

THE PEOPLE WE LOVE REMAIN
Henry, O. *The Gift of the Magi*. Simon & Schuster, 1997.

MUDDYING WALDEN
Kimball, Kristen. *The Dirty Life: A Memoir of Farming, Food and Love*. Scribner, 2011.
Schulz, Kathryn. "Why Do We Love Henry David Thoreau?" *The New Yorker*. 19 October 2015
Thoreau, Henry David. *Walden & On the Duty of Civil Disobedience*. Holt, Rinehart and Winston, 1966.

꒰ꔧ꒱

ACKNOWLEDGMENTS

Much like a year of no buying, writing a book is best undertaken with the love and support of those around you. It is with profound gratitude that I wish to thank: my first and best believers, Arthur and Jacqueline Quern, Margaret Quern Atkins; my writing mentors and coaches – Juliana Thibodeaux, Deborah Siegel, Eula Biss, Janna Maron (along with the rest of the MTTS community); those who provided the space for me to write – The Ragdale Foundation, David and Jennifer Wood and the staff of Glencoe Union Church; those who protected my time – Jenny Richards, the Misters Pratt; my early draft readers – Linda Pratt, Adam Davis, Katie Macrae Lasky, Liza Greville, Eula Biss, David Wood, Kaethe Morris Hoffer, Jacqueline Quern; those who saw merit in initial versions of these essays – editors at *The Waking* (the *Ruminate Magazine* blog), *BioStories, Chicago Parent;* those who believed in the collection as a whole – the editors at EastOver Press; and, finally, Walter Robinson whose wise and gentle counsel shepherded this project from manuscript to book.

Finally, there would be no book without John, Oliver, Foster, and Elliot Pratt, who were game enough to go along with my hare-brained scheme and generous enough to let me write about it. In case it isn't clear by now, they are the absolute best.

CPSIA information can be obtained
at www.ICGtesting.com
Printed in the USA
LVHW101639090722
723112LV00004B/330